W9-BRU-865

RETURN
with
HONOR

RETURN with HONOR

CAPTAIN SCOTT O'GRADY
WITH JEFF COPLON

Thorndike Press • Chivers Press
Thorndike, Maine USA   Bath, Avon, England

This Large Print edition is published by Thorndike Press, USA and by Chivers Press, England.

Published in 1996 in the U.S. by arrangement with Doubleday, a division of Bantam Doubleday Dell Publishing Group, Inc.

Published in 1996 in the U.K. by arrangement with Doubleday, a division of Bantam Doubleday Dell Publishing Group, Inc.

U.S. Hardcover 0-7862-0676-4 (Basic Series Edition)
U.K. Hardcover 0-7451-5330-5 (Windsor Large Print)

Thorndike Large Print ® Basic Series.

The text of this Large Print edition is unabridged.
Other aspects of the book may vary from the original edition.

Set in 16 pt. News Plantin by Juanita Macdonald.

Printed in the United States on permanent paper.

British Library Cataloguing in Publication Data available

Library of Congress Cataloging in Publication Data

O'Grady, Scott.
    Return with honor / Scott O'Grady ; with Jeff Coplon.
      p.   cm.
    ISBN 0-7862-0676-4 (lg. print : hc)
    1. O'Grady, Scott. 2. Yugoslav War, 1991– — Aerial
operations, American. 3. Yugoslav War, 1991– — Personal
narratives, American. 4. Yugoslav War, 1991– — Bosnia and
Hercegovina. 5. Bosnia and Hercegovina — History, Military.
6. Military pilots — United States — Biography. 7. Military pilots
— Bosnia and Hercegovina — Biography. I. Coplon, Jeff.
II. Title.
DR1313.7.A47O38   1996
949.702'4—dc20   96-6178

To all the men and women who have served in the U.S. military, with our NATO allies, or with the U.N. peace-keeping forces.

And, most of all, to our POWs and MIAs, past and present.

I want to thank God for the gift of another shot at life.

— S.O.

"*I knew, wherever I was, that you thought of me, and if I got in a tight place, you would come.*"

— GENERAL SHERMAN TO GENERAL GRANT

CODE OF CONDUCT

I I am an American, fighting in the forces which guard my country and our way of life. I am prepared to give my life in their defense.

II I will never surrender of my own free will. If in command, I will never surrender the members of my command while they still have the means to resist.

III If I am captured I will continue to resist by all means available. I will make every effort to escape and aid others to escape. I will accept neither parole nor special favors from the enemy.

IV If I become a prisoner of war, I will keep faith with my fellow prisoners. I will give no information or take part in any action which might be harmful to my comrades. If I am senior, I will take command. If not, I will obey the lawful orders of those appointed over me and will back them up in every way.

V When questioned, should I become a prisoner of war, I am required to give name, rank, service number, and date of birth. I will evade answering further questions to the utmost of my ability. I will make no oral or written statements disloyal to my country and its allies or harmful to their cause.

VI I will never forget that I am an American, fighting for freedom, responsible for my actions, and dedicated to the principles which made my country free. I will trust in my God and in the United States of America.

ACKNOWLEDGMENTS

Scott O'Grady and Jeff Coplon would like to thank Master Sergeant Bruce Townsend and his colleagues at the Joint Services SERE Agency; Michael Grost and his hardworking staff at the U.S. Air Force Life Sciences Equipment Laboratory at Kelly Air Force Base; General Ronald Sconyers, Major Chris Geisel, and all the helpful people at Air Force public affairs; Arlene Friedman, publisher of Doubleday, for her vision and enthusiasm in bringing this book into being; David Gernert, Doubleday's editor in chief, who brought our writing team together and pushed all the right buttons; Bill Thomas, our editor, who kept us in line and on time; editorial assistant Jacqueline LaPierre, who worked beyond the call to help us make our deadlines; and Esther Newberg and Michael Carlisle, our agents, for their guidance and support.

HIGH FLIGHT

by John Gillespie Magee, Jr.

Oh, I have slipped the surly bonds of earth
And danced the skies on laughter-silvered
    wings;
Sunward I've climbed, and joined the tum-
    bling mirth
Of sun-split clouds — and done a hundred
    things
You have not dreamed of — wheeled and
    soared and swung
High in the sunlit silence. Hov'ring there,
I've chased the shouting wind along, and flung
My eager craft through footless halls of air.
Up, up the long, delirious, burning blue
I've topped the windswept heights with easy
    grace,
Where never lark, or even eagle flew.
And, while with silent, lifting mind I've trod
The high untrespassed sanctity of space,
Put out my hand, and touched the face of God.

CHAPTER ONE

Weeks later, after it was all over — after I'd been shot out of the sky, stalked like prey, and welcomed back like someone home from the dead — I'd joke that we could blame the whole thing on Brick Izzi.

Captain Izzi was one of my fellow F-16 pilots with the 555th Fighter Squadron, the "Triple Nickel," at Aviano Air Base in northeastern Italy. He was a good friend, a guy I'd known since pilot training, and he also served as a squadron scheduling officer. That week his task was to coordinate our Operation Deny Flight missions over Bosnia. For more than a year, the Triple Nickel's thirty-five pilots had been part of NATO's effort to maintain Bosnian airspace as a no-fly zone for any and all combatants.

It was Thursday, June 1, and I'd just returned to Aviano from a week's duty at the Combined Air Operations Center (CAOC) in Vicenza, the NATO nerve center for Deny

Flight. That was also the day I officially became life support officer for the 555th, and I was working double-time to learn the ropes at my new shop. On top of flying, Air Force pilots have what we call "additional duties" — sixty-hour-a-week jobs in operations, training, safety, weapons, or some other vital function. My job was to help out the six enlisted personnel who actually ran the shop and took care of our squadron's parachutes, ejection seats, and survival gear.

I dropped by the scheduling shop that morning to see where I was slotted that week. Brick turned to me and said, "Hey, Scott, you want to fly tomorrow with Wilbur, or do you want me to put you on ground alert?" He knew I was busy at life support. On ground alert, an on-call status, I'd be able to stay at my shop and leave Deny Flight to others — unless something came up and they needed to scramble us into action.

"But hey, you know," Brick said mischievously, "you fly this one day and you get a hundred and fifty bucks."

While U.S. pilots weren't credited for combat time over Bosnia, they did get hazardous-flight pay — $150 per calendar month, whether they flew there one day out of the month or thirty. The 555th participated in Deny Flight for about half the year; we alternated with the 510th, our sister squadron at the 31st Fighter Wing in Aviano. On our off months we were deployed back to the States or to one of our NATO allies. The 510th was set to take over Deny Flight for most of June. But the Triple Nickel's assignment ran through the first two days of that month, which meant that our pilots could earn a little bonus with a single run.

Now, you need to understand that Brick was joking with me here — we both knew the extra cash was no big deal. I wanted to fly that Thursday because I hadn't flown for two weeks and because flying is what I do. I'd logged about eight hundred hours in the F-16, and the plane still thrilled me as much as it had the first time, four years before.

The most experienced F-16 pilots learn something new each time out. There's no way to know it all; there's no such thing as a perfect flight. You can always find room for improvement, and it's a constant battle just to maintain your proficiency. The longer you're out of the cockpit, the tougher it is to stay on top of your game.

So I was itching to fly. Period. But grabbing a quick buck and a half — for what had come to be a routine mission — didn't hurt.

"Put me on," I told Brick.

That was all there was to it. I'd signed up

r another day at the office, no more and
o less.

I had no way of knowing that this particular
routine mission would change the course of
my life.

Aviano was thirty minutes from the beach,
thirty minutes from the mountains, and thirty
minutes from a Balkan civil war. I lived in
Montereale Val Cellina, a nearby village at the
base of the Italian Alps; drive ten minutes
north and you were looking at a scene out
of *Heidi*. Montereale wasn't a big town, but
it had five or six fantastic restaurants, and I
could fall out of bed into a friendly café. I'd
come to admire the Italian lifestyle, where
people took the time to enjoy their families
and friends and mealtimes together. My land-
lords, the Lovisas, lived upstairs, and they
treated me like a grandson.

I'd called twenty-six places home in the past
eleven years, but Montereale was just about
the sweetest.

Thursday morning I woke up and did my
"S's" — showered and shaved. I passed on
breakfast; all I had in the fridge was a bottle
of wine, half a loaf of bread, and a box of
frozen corn. I climbed into my flight suit, a
drab-green jumpsuit that zippered from
crotch to neck, and grabbed my wallet and

14

logbook. I hopped into my Toyota 4Runner for the twenty-minute drive to Aviano, along a country road past sprouting cornfields.

I was crazy about the Toyota, which was as big a truck as the narrow Italian streets allowed. I'd bought it after totaling my BMW the previous September. I have this bad habit with cars — I've wrecked about every one I've owned, and a few that I haven't, beginning with my parents' Chevy Suburban back in Spokane, Washington. But the BMW was the topper. I'd been on my way to work before dawn that morning, on this same country road. It was pitch-dark, and as I steered into a bend, the lights from an oncoming car momentarily blinded me.

Suddenly I realized I was in the oncoming lane, and I jerked on the wheel. My correction spun out the BMW's back end, throwing me sideways down the road and off into the left-hand ditch. I mowed down a row of small trees and rolled over one and a half times, waiting to pass out or worse. I ended upside down, still clutching the wheel.

The air bag had inflated, saving my eyes from the shattered glass. But it was the seat belt that spared the rest of me. Every surface of that car was squashed. Everything not bolted down had flown out.

I crawled out and stood by the side of the

road. As far as I could tell, I had a small scratch on my hand and a slightly sore neck, but nothing more. About two minutes later an Italian guy who worked at the base drove up and stopped. He stepped up to the remains of the BMW and peered inside, certain that anyone there was surely done for.

"Hey, I'm over here!" I called out.

The man started and came up to me, wide-eyed. He touched my cheek and stared, as if looking at a ghost.

When I told my family about that little accident, we agreed that I'd used up at least one of my nine lives.

A few minutes before ten, I produced my ID card at the main gate, then swung west down the flight line to where our airplanes were sitting. I showed my line badge at a second security checkpoint, parked the truck, and entered the squadron building. I checked in at the operations, or "ops," desk to confirm my mission and schedule, and then I met up with Bob "Wilbur" Wright.

For both tactical and safety reasons, F-16 pilots never fly alone. At Aviano we usually went out in "two-ship" elements, with one other plane; at other times we were part of a four-ship. As flight lead for our two-ship this afternoon, Wilbur would be in charge of tactics, navigation, communications, and keeping tabs on the weather. I'd back him up as wingman. The casting might easily have been reversed, as both of us were qualified to fly the lead. But on a given sortie you could only have one chief.

I'd known Wilbur and his wife, Sharon, since we'd served together at Kunsan Air Base in Korea in 1992. Wilbur was an athletic guy who'd played baseball at the Air Force Academy — a lot more athletic than me. He was also highly respected as a pilot and an officer, a conscientious pro. Weaker pilots get weeded out before reaching a place like Aviano, but there are always degrees of excellence. Wilbur ranked in the upper tier.

To the extent that fighter pilots share a personality profile, it's 180 degrees removed from the Tom Cruise character in *Top Gun*. You won't find flamboyant, hotshot biker types in an F-16 squadron. We need to master a Ph.D.'s worth of knowledge, from flying procedures and tactics to threat capabilities and weapon systems, and to do our jobs we'd better be mature and self-disciplined about it. In Aviano I was one of the younger pilots at twenty-nine; we had more than a few balding types with station wagons and a bunch of screaming kids in the back. Wilbur was thirty-three years old; he and Sharon were expecting a child in July, and I knew how excited they were about that.

Let me put it another way: F-16 pilots, as a group, are normal people with abnormal responsibilities. They love to fly, no question. But they also want to make the world a better place, a safer place. They are people who want to make a difference.

Wilbur and I walked into one of the small briefing rooms. It wasn't much: a table, a few chairs, a chalkboard, a VCR. Each time we flew we'd put in a tape to record our video displays, along with the audio from our radio and intercom. It was a great tool for debriefing.

Briefing was the flight lead's job; the wingman was there to listen and jot notes for any questions at the end. With some key points already on the chalkboard, Wilbur opened his written guide and jumped in. It was a typical Wilbur Wright briefing: fast-paced, thorough, well organized. I'd racked up forty-six Deny Flight sorties over Bosnia, at least four of them with Wilbur, but I knew that each one was different. While precision standards govern the flying of an F-16, they're dynamic and flexible. After you'd laid off for several days, as I had, a refresher course was welcome.

Wilbur began with the basic objectives for our mission. That part was straightforward.

We were in Bosnia to back up U.N. peace-keepers on the ground and to enforce the no-fly zone. Our goal: to prevent anyone from using the air median to project military power against other warring factions. We were flying not in support of the Bosnian government, but to uphold U.N. Security Council resolutions. We'd be watching for violators from *any* side — Serb, Croat, Muslim, it made no difference.

As professional warriors, neither Wilbur nor I nor anyone else at Aviano had a political stake in this situation. The politicians made the decisions and gave the orders. It was our job, assuming those orders were lawful, to carry them out.

We'd been "fragged" for a standard four-to-six hour patrol. We'd be operating in the northwest corner of Bosnia, near Bihac, rather than roaming throughout the entire area of responsibility, as was often the case. Bosnia was a small country, with a potpourri of NATO forces flying over it: French Mirages, Dutch F-16s, British Harriers, U.S. Navy F-18s. Our F-16 missions were orchestrated with theirs, both for tactics and to make sure that no one bumped heads.

Wilbur proceeded to run through the "motherhood," the basic principles for every sortie. He covered our operating standards, our "contracts" as flight lead and wingman, our radio procedures, our contingency and emergency plans — what we'd do, for example, if our engine quit or if we got shot down. He ticked off the weapons we'd be hauling that day, stationed under the wings and body of our aircraft: two air-to-air missiles and two laser-guided bombs sat our under wing pylons; two more air-to-air missiles on our wingtips; a 20-mm Gatling gun mounted in the fuselage; and an electronic countermeasures pod, fixed to each plane's belly, to jam enemy radar.

There's a lot to discuss before a mission; it can take a solid hour to do it right. At the very end, Wilbur covered our squadron's search-and-rescue procedures, known as SAR, for recovering downed airmen in combat areas. In the typical preflight briefing, this would amount to a three-minute generic outline — a skeleton plan, like the note you'd leave on your dashboard before heading off to camp in the woods.

While I'd glanced at our written SAR material some weeks before, it wasn't something I'd spent much time studying. In the real world, pilots can't map out escape and evasion ploys in advance. There are too many variables outside your control, from terrain and injuries to the proximity of hostile forces. In the real world you have to improvise, to adjust to shifting circumstances, to fall back on common sense and the first-rate survival training every Air Force pilot receives.

There were general SAR principles in Aviano that every pilot signed off on, but we also had the latitude to make minor changes from one sortie to the next. For some unknown reason, Wilbur went into extensive detail on his individual SAR plan that day, taking twice as long as normal. When he asked me for mine, I took the ball and ran with it.

"First I'll get out of my parachute and get away, and find a hiding place for my stuff, so don't be afraid if you don't hear from me for a while," I began. "Then I'll come up and talk on the radio on Guard [the international distress channel] — I'll want the whole world to know I'm alive.

"After that, I'll fix my location on GPS [global positioning system, a satellite-aided navigational device], and I'll come up on Alpha to tell them my coordinates." Alpha was one of two search-and-rescue channels on our handheld radios. While not electronically secure, its "freq," or frequency, was classified on a need-to-know basis and changed regularly. Alpha definitely offered more privacy than Guard, to which everyone and his cousin would be listening — including, it was safe to bet, the people we'd be running from.

For added security, I gave Wilbur a letter code I'd devised for my GPS coordinates. I'd log the code on a sheet of paper on my knee board, to be strapped to my body in the plane.

"But what if you lose the paper?" Wilbur said.

Good question. I thought a minute and came up with a paper-free backup for storing the code.

That was about it for my plan. It wouldn't have done Wilbur or me any good to go further, to agonize over things beyond predicting; we'd only have been distracted from our mission. F-16 pilots aren't trained to get shot down; we're trained to defend ourselves, and to take out the *other* guy. We're taught to be aggressive, to use our state-of-the-art airplane to its fullest capacity — to treat the sky as our domain.

At the same time, we're also well schooled to evade and survive if the need arises. There's a lot of time and energy and funding invested in a fighter pilot, and the Air Force doesn't take our lives lightly.

In sum, I wasn't dwelling on survival scenarios as I got ready to go up that day. In all my sorties over Bosnia, the most action I'd had was to buzz over some low-flying helicopters, to intimidate them into compliance.

As far as I knew, I'd never been fired on with so much as a cap gun.

No U.S. fighter pilot had been shot down since Operation Desert Storm in 1991. After more than a year of Deny Flight over Bosnia, hostile ground fire had taken down but one plane, a British Harrier, whose pilot was returned by local Muslims the same day. While I knew that lots of people on Bosnian soil didn't like us, I wasn't planning to be victim number two.

Just after noon, Wilbur and I moved into a secure area for our intelligence brief — a quick update, like headline news, of any late-breaking troop movements. The intel officer had nothing significant to report, but the shop's enlisted personnel shared their prosciutto and mushroom pizza, my first meal of the day.

We all knew that things were getting worse on the ground, a lot worse. During my week in Vicenza, NATO had called in air strikes against a munitions depot in the Bosnian Serb stronghold of Pale. In retaliation, the Bosnian Serbs had taken more than 350 peacekeepers hostage and stepped up their attacks against designated "safe areas," including the Bosnian capital of Sarajevo. The humanitarian airlift had been down for months; no emergency food convoys had made it through in two weeks.

To top it off, the Bosnian Serbs were making noises about shooting down one of our planes. It wasn't the first time they'd made that threat. But it did cinch the tension up a notch.

We'd never regarded Deny Flight as a Sunday spin in the country. We knew that ground-based threats were everywhere in Bosnia. The country was filled to bursting with portable weapons, from small arms to antiaircraft artillery to the shoulder-propped, heat-seeking missiles known as SA-7s, or "man-pads," one of which knocked down the British Harrier.

More troublesome still were the powerful, battery-loaded SA-6s, which could deliver as many as three radar-guided, surface-to-air missiles, or SAMs, with much bigger payloads. An SA-7 is to an SA-6 what a tricycle is to a Lamborghini.

When Yugoslavia fell apart, the Bosnian Serb army inherited a modern, Soviet-built air defense system. According to our intelligence, most of their SAM sites were concentrated around Bihac and near Banja Luka, in north-central Bosnia. We'd confirmed frequent radar emissions from air defense sites in those areas, all of them north of a line around the 45th parallel.

Fighter pilots continually adjust tactics to threats, as well as work within their theater's rules of engagement. The rules protect both the pilots and noncombatants below and help prevent unplanned escalations. We never John Wayne it in an F-16; we don't rush out there with our six-shooters to take on anyone who wants a piece of us.

Wilbur and I would be staying south of that danger line during our mission that afternoon. We had no call for any package of escort planes, no reason to expect anything unusual.

There was just one catch: SA-6 batteries are mobile. They can be hauled on the sly to just about anywhere. Yes, Wilbur and I would play by the rules. But there was no guarantee we'd stay out of harm's way.

We stopped back with the administrative folks at the ops desk for a one-minute "step brief," to check our airfield status and find out where our planes were sitting — they'd been moved from their hardened shelters some time before. There were no maintenance delays, and the sky looked fine, with scattered clouds and no storms in sight.

Then Wilbur asked me to verify my search-and-rescue plan — an unexpected question, what with all the other things we were thinking about. "I just want to make sure I understand what you'll do if you have to eject," he said. I ran it down again, and he seemed satisfied.

From there we walked from the "hard side" to the "soft side" of our squadron building, to the locker room in our life support shop, where we'd dress for the mission. We sanitized our flight suits, removing the blue and yellow Velcro patches from the Triple Nickel (a fierce bald eagle) and the 31st Fighter Wing (a winged dragon). If captured, we didn't want the bad guys to know what units we were from; name, rank, serial number, and date of birth, and that was it.

With my Swiss Army knife stowed in my chest pocket, I put on my G-suit, a moss-green girdle that fit over my lower torso. Next came my survival vest, zipped over my upper body, my GPS receiver stuck in the inside right pocket.

I procured my 9-mm semiautomatic Beretta, loaded a clip of fifteen bullets, and holstered the gun, on safety, under my left armpit. A second clip was stashed in my G-suit's right shin pocket, along with an evasion map and my blood chit — a promissory note from the government to reward anyone aiding a U.S. service man in distress. (My chit was printed in eleven languages, including Serbian and Serbo-Croatian.)

I buckled on my parachute harness, another thin layer of fire-resistant material, over my vest. Then I placed my helmet in a cloth helmet bag, along with my lineup card, which listed our mission number, takeoff time, call signs, and the designated Alpha frequency. I checked for my earplugs and my flashlight.

By 12:30 P.M. Wilbur and I were making tracks for the flight line when it hit me — I'd forgotten my flight jacket, still hanging on a peg in my locker. I'd never left it behind on a sortie before, but I let it go. I wasn't in the mood to wrestle my vest off and back on again, and our planes were ready.

I'd be all right, I told myself. We've got a terrific climate control system in the F-16 — you can dial up any temperature you want. And even though it was cool outside, even though we'd been taught to "dress to egress," I just didn't think that I'd be ejecting that day.

I hopped into a van and motored out to my aircraft. After trading greetings with my crew chief, I asked him how the plane had been flying and looked over the aircraft forms: everything was go. Standing by was the fire guard with his big green bottle, just in case my engine caught on fire when I started up. I'd never heard of that happening with an F-16, but I knew that every Air Force safety procedure had some history behind it — that something bad had happened at least once before. The idea was

27

to keep it from happening again.

I walked around and eyeballed that sleek, gunmetal-gray, forty-seven-foot plane. You take nothing for granted on a sortie; I made sure the right weapons were loaded, double-checked the oil and tires. Then I climbed the ladder hanging from the cockpit and perched on the canopy rail. I anchored my left hand on the left ledge, reached to the opposite side with my right, and swung my legs into the foot wells, as if hopping into a convertible. My legs now straddled the center instrument console; my feet were planted on the rudder pedals. I was in place, ready to strap in.

I snapped my G-suit into an air hose, to swell the suit's five bladders — two on each leg, one at my stomach — and help stop my blood from pooling under high gravitational forces. I hooked the harness clips at my shoulders to my parachute risers, which also functioned as shoulder belts. Two more clips linked my hips to a canvas-padded seat kit; stored inside were my life raft, my survival gear rucksack, and a smaller, "hit-and-run" survival kit. The whole package was contained within the hardened seat pan on which I sat.

With my lap belt pulled tight, I put on my helmet and secured my oxygen mask. The mask, a new model called Combat Edge, was designed to help us breathe under high

G-forces. It was less comfortable than the old type, and I liked to leave it a little loose — I could tighten it quickly if the going got rough.

"Rail clear?" the crew chief called.

I replied with a thumbs-up and a nod of my head, making sure my elbows were safe inside. After the crew chief pulled the ladder from the plane, I held down a spring-loaded switch on the front cockpit wall. An aerodynamic bubble canopy lowered into place, as smoothly as the windows in a Lexus, and locked automatically. I activated the canopy seal for cabin pressurization.

The canopy was a marvel in itself. Crafted out of space-age polycarbonate, it worked as cover and windscreen at the same time. What's more, it offered a spectacular solution to the age-old aviation bugaboo of bird strikes. When an F-16 intersected a bird's path at up to around 500 miles per hour, the canopy would not shatter like those of cast acrylic. Instead, it would flow and bend, absorbing the impact, before snapping back to its original form; the bird — very dead by that point — simply rippled across it. This is why F-16 pilots keep a fist-high space between canopy and top of head: if they brush up too close, they might get bashed by a seagull-sized depression.

I set up my knee boards, two cloth clipboards with pens and notepads and my lineup card. I secured them with Velcro straps around my thighs, then set my switches to their start positions. For me, the thrill of piloting an F-16 started right there, well before takeoff. I'm five-foot-eight, and the cockpit fit me real snug — I don't know how the bigger pilots manage to squeeze themselves in. It's a unique sensation: you strap yourself into other planes, but you strap an F-16 *upon* you, *around* you, till it's an extension of your body and mind, as sensitive as a thin leather glove.

The crew chief came up on my intercom, and I asked if all was ready: "Fore and aft clear; fire guard posted; chocks in place?"

"Roger," the crew chief came back at me. "All ready for run-up."

I flicked on two switches: the first for electrical power, the second to activate the jet fuel starter, a small engine that generates the torque to turn over the main motor, the GE-100, one of the best jet engines in the world. I clutched the throttle with my left hand and advanced it from off to idle; the engine surged to life.

Next came the ground checks, when I brought the aircraft's systems on-line, one by one. You could do this very quickly if you had to, but the crew chief and I had no reason to rush that day, and we took twenty minutes to complete the process. I fed my current latitude and longitude into the inertial navigation system, a gyro-stabilized platform for my instruments. Using this initial reference point, the INS would give me distances and bearings to any point throughout my flight.

I checked the round dial instruments on my center console: speed, altitude, and attitude (the plane's reference to the horizon), plus my horizontal situation indicator, an electronic compass. To the left, just over my knee, an airborne radar screen would flag any no-fly zone violators; above that, my threat warning system would alert me to hostile radar.

Atop the console sat a rectangular keyboard pad and the buttons for our two radios. Crowning the whole shooting match was my head-up display, a transparent glass panel that reads out data for navigation and weapons targeting.

When our two-ship was ready to taxi, I confirmed that my feet were holding the brakes and signaled thumbs-out. The fire guard removed the chocks from my landing gear and stood clear. The crew chief gave me a "run-up" sign, with second and third fingers extended — the old Cub Scout salute — and tracing circles in the air. Then he directed me forward, waving both hands back past his ears.

Falling in behind Wilbur, I nudged the throttle briefly past idle, to taxi out toward the runway, working my rudder pedals to steer. Just before taking the runway, we stopped for a final systems check by the end-of-runway crew. Weapon troops pulled the safeties on my missiles and bombs. I kept my hands open and high, where the ground crew could see them throughout; one careless touch of a flight control can knock a guy flat or worse when he's underneath your plane.

We were cleared for takeoff. As we taxied onto the runway, I took my position just up-wind of Wilbur, so that his jet wash and exhaust would blow off the runway and away from me. I leaned back my head till it touched my seat's headrest, then swung my chin forward to my chest: an exaggerated nod, to signal I was ready. I watched Wilbur, who was listening for clearance from the air traffic control tower. Soon enough he gave me another run-up signal. With my feet on the brakes, I pushed the throttle to an upper midrange setting, 90 percent power. Time for one last check on my engine and hydraulic systems, one last look for any caution or warning lights. With my right hand on the stick — essentially a three-dimensional joystick, with several inset function buttons — I cycled my flight controls, triple-checking for the smallest hiccup. All was in order.

I looked up again and gave one more big nod — and then I watched Wilbur take off, with a burn and a roar, a spectacle that always stirred me. As I waited with my engine cooking, he bore down the runway at full thrust. His engine nozzle opened and a long flame shot back; his afterburner had kicked in. I heard the rumbling and my plane shook, as from a minor earthquake. Wilbur got smaller in a hurry, till the flame was a red dot.

Twenty seconds after he'd started — a separation we use to avert any risk of colliding — it was my turn. I took my feet off the brakes and advanced the throttle to full "military power." I heard the engine rise in pitch, and then, with a glance at my instruments, I moved the throttle to full afterburner, the max. Now I was injecting fuel directly into a hot exhaust stream, creating enormous thrust — just the ticket for taking off with a heavy payload in the shortest possible runway space.

I felt the kick of the afterburner and the exhilaration of sheer speed as my plane hurtled down the runway. If you've ever raced a drag car, you'd have a rough sense of it; my plane might trail a dragster for the first eighth of a mile or so, but after that, rest assured, it would smoke him. Taking off in an F-16 is like sitting on a controlled explosion.

As I reached 90 miles an hour, I disconnected my nosewheel steering, since the rudder now had enough airflow to guide the plane. Within 3,000 feet I'd reached takeoff speed, around 200 miles an hour; a touch of back pressure on the stick jumped my plane into the air. I made lightning dial checks of attitude, altitude, and vertical velocity — all on the mark. The flight-path marker on my head-up display confirmed that I was climbing properly. There would be no abort. The jet was accelerating at a phenomenal rate now, and my next reflex was to retract my landing gear before it reached its damage threshold of 330 miles per hour.

It was 1:15 P.M. Aviano time, and I was away.

We proceeded along our standard departure routing, chosen to satisfy concerns about airspace, traffic control, and noise abatement for surrounding towns. At 350 miles per hour, I disengaged the afterburner and reverted to full military power.

Pilots follow this sequence: first you aviate, then you navigate, then you communicate. Once I felt confident that my plane was flying right, I locked onto Wilbur with my radar. I fixed my airspeed and direction to follow twenty seconds — some two miles — behind him. Once my trail was set, I radioed to Wilbur on our interflight frequency, using the wingman's flight position number: "Two is tied."

I pierced a broken cloud deck at 12,000 feet, saw nothing but clear sky ahead. "Two is visual," I called.

"Clear to rejoin," he replied. Wilbur had already cut back a notch on his throttle, and I closed the gap with geometry, angling at him at full military power. By that time we were over the Adriatic, the clear blue channel that divides Italy and the Balkans.

The wingman serves as a two-ship's lookout, using eyes and radar both. But his main responsibility is to hold his flight position — to sustain the formation chosen by the flight lead. That afternoon we rejoined in a fingertip formation, where I held within five feet of Wilbur's wingtip. There's nothing magical about this — you learn the skills in basic pilot training, and after a time it's like riding a bicycle.

While close-in, Wilbur and I conducted a leak and panel check of each other's planes, to be sure the aircraft structures were shipshape. We tested our on-board defensive systems by expending flares and chaff, the foil sheets used to decoy enemy radar and divert incoming missiles. Then, with a jiggle of his stick, Wilbur porpoised the nose of his jet up and down. That was my signal to move into a standard formation, "tactical line abreast": a mile and a half apart, with an altitude stack of 1,000 to 2,000 feet. I veered off and found my spot.

Soon we'd crossed over the notched Croatian coast and past the lush, green river gorge that forms part of the boundary between Croatia and Bosnia. We set up shop for our first "vul time" (short for vulnerability time) over Bosnian hill country, southeast of Bihac, 27,000 feet up. The F-16 can scorch the sky at more than twice the speed of sound, but we rarely need that kind of velocity; today we'd be cruising at around 400 miles per hour.

Wilbur established an oval pattern for our combat air patrol, or "cap," a racetrack-shaped course we'd follow for the duration. Each leg of the oval was twenty-five miles long, about three minutes' travel. We'd take another minute to bank our way in tandem through a 180-degree, clockwise turn; then run a three-minute return leg and a second turn, to get back to where we'd started.

We could have made those turns sharper, but we weren't auditioning for the Thunderbirds. On a mission like Deny Flight, fighter pilots worked on two levels: the administrative (navigation, contracts, formations) and the tactical. Our aim was to keep the administrative side as simple as possible, to better concentrate on patrolling — and on using our weapons as necessary.

Not long after reaching our cap point, we detected a low-flying aircraft several miles to the west, near the Udbina airfield. Udbina was a base for the Krajanian Serbs, who then controlled a chunk of eastern Croatia. We'd crossed swords with them back in February 1994, after they launched an air strike against Muslim sites in midwestern Bosnia. NATO forces intercepted them and shot four of their planes down.

For now we'd just keep an eye on the plane, making sure it respected the no-fly zone.

Wilbur and I kept making those diligent eight-minute ovals, but the work never got boring. The F-16 owns the ultimate in cab-forward, user-friendly design; virtually all of the plane lies below and behind you. The cockpit, the pilot's office, is laid out to keep your head up and your hands on the throttle and side-stick controller. The one-piece canopy, the only one of its kind, lets your eyes roam unobstructed. Throw in an ergonomic seat, tilted back at a thirty-degree angle, plus the insulation of your earplugs and ear cuff pads, and you can't help but feel a part of the sky. On top of the world.

That's a high that's hard to match.

At about 2:30 P.M. we went to take a "dip" — to refuel — on an airborne tanker; we'd need to go twice during a typical mission. Ending our first vul time, we zipped back over the Adriatic and found our gigantic flying gas station, a customized Boeing 707. After slowing to 330 miles an hour, I parked on the tanker's wing while Wilbur was serviced. It took seven minutes to replenish his tanks with jet fuel, that combustive mix of gasoline and kerosene.

Then Wilbur came up on the wing and I dropped below the 707's huge belly. An operator lowered a boom at the tanker's tail and plugged it into my air refueling door, just behind the cockpit at the top of the plane. While you're refueling you can chat with the tanker crew over your intercom, and I passed the time of day. But it wasn't until we were shoving off that Wilbur mentioned that he'd found a former "Juvat" among the crew, a pilot with the 80th Fighter Squadron in Korea.

That was big news — like bumping into an old fraternity brother halfway across the globe. I'd belonged to three squadrons in my Air Force career, and was proud of them all, but my time in Korea was special. The squadron coin, the token carried by every pilot from the 80th till the day he died, said it all: "You

38

will always be a JUVAT no matter where you go."

As we left the tanker, I couldn't resist tuning back to the tanker's frequency. "Basher Five-Two is up your freq," I said, giving my call sign for that day's mission.

"What can we do for you?" a crewman answered.

"I hear you have a Juvat on board," I said.

A different voice broke in, with a warmer tone to it: "Yeah, that would be me!"

I needed no more prompting to recite my old squadron's Latin motto: *Audentes fortuna juvat* ("Fortune favors the bold").

"Thanks a lot, bud," the former fighter pilot replied. "I'll see you here again real soon."

We flew east back toward Bihac for our second vul time, the middle segment of our mission. To get out of some high clouds and make our work more efficient, Wilbur led us a few miles to the north and better weather. He made sure to stay outside the SAM threat rings, while remaining east of the border with Croatia. Airspace was cramped for Deny Flight.

We resumed our oval cap patterns in tactical line abreast, with Wilbur a thousand feet below me. In our first vul time our legs had run northwest and southeast; now we'd rotated toward due west and east.

We had no reason to suspect anything unusual. We had no way of knowing, in particular, that a Bosnian Serb outfit had secretly tractored an SA-6 battery south. Or that it had lined up its missiles just east of our patrol area, within easy range, poised to pounce — to down the first U.S. pilot in the course of this long and ugly war.

The first hint that this sortie might be different came minutes later, when Wilbur's threat warning system told him he was "spiked" — that an enemy radar on the ground might be looking at him.

In a place like Bosnia, radar was about as common as air pollution. On the most basic level you had broad-beamed search radars, general tracking instruments which registered everyone out there, not so different from traffic control screens at Kennedy Airport or LAX. NATO hadn't bombed search radar sites in Bosnia.

But Wilbur's warning signal showed that he'd been pinpointed by a tracking, or "acquisition," radar — a threat radar, the kind associated with surface-to-air missiles. An acquisition radar looks at a single aircraft — examines it through a soda straw — to gather data for a missile launcher.

Wilbur's alert didn't mean they were actually shooting at him, but they sure might be thinking about it.

"Basher Five-One, mud six, bearing zero-nine-zero," Wilbur called out over our open frequency: possible threat radar to the east.

I briskly chimed in, "Basher Five-Two naked"; I hadn't picked anything up.

Then we listened for Magic, NATO's airborne early warning platform, the widest eyes in the sky. We knew that Magic was polling other agencies to determine if the threat was real. It seemed likely that Wilbur's warning had been triggered by radar from one of the known SAM rings to the north and northeast of us, which was no sweat. They could track us all they wanted, but they couldn't hurt us outside their missiles' range.

After ten seconds of dead air, Magic responded, "Basher Five-One, your mud six report is uncorrelated."

A false alarm. Full speed ahead.

Not long after Wilbur's scare, at exactly three minutes after three o'clock, it happened. We were on an eastbound leg when I heard an alarm from my radar warning receiver over my headset. I confirmed it on my threat warning screen: acquisition radar, due east. I was spiked.

"Basher Five-Two, mud six, bearing zero-nine-zero," I rang out.

41

"Basher Five-One naked," Wilbur replied.

As I monitored for Magic to weigh in, I ran through the facts as I knew them. To begin with, the indication might be spurious, from a source that mimicked an SA-6 site. Or it might come from one of those out-of-range SAM rings; the due-east bearing supported that theory, and so did Wilbur's recent warning.

On the other hand, no intelligence was failsafe, and it was humanly impossible to keep track of every mobile antiaircraft weapon in Bosnia.

You might say I felt uneasy. I didn't like being stared at — especially when the staring might preface a ballistic payload, aimed straight at my gut. I gazed out through my panoramic canopy, scanning 180 degrees, while maintaining my visual formation with Wilbur. I watched for the telltale white smoke plume of an SA-6's rocket motor, before the rocket shuts off and the missile glides on, at supersonic speed . . .

I didn't see a thing.

Five seconds after the spike, my audio warning signal shut off, as programmed, but the video stayed on my screen: a possible threat was still out there.

Six seconds after the spike, I heard a new signal, louder and pulsing, more like a car alarm. Heart sinking, I looked back at my screen. I had a new warning there as well, brighter than the one before.

I'd just gotten the worst news a pilot can get — I'd been locked up by a target-tracking radar, the type that guides a missile to its mark. There wasn't much hope of a false alarm at this stage. Someone was shooting at me.

The missile might already be in the air.

My first thought was angry and simple: *We've been set up.* They'd laid a trap for us, and all of our detection systems had missed it. I was swimming straight into the jaws of the shark.

I didn't care what Magic might report to me at this point. I had better information than they did — I *knew* what was happening out there. And I knew, too, that I had only myself to rely on. It was my little pink body on the line, and no radio call would make that missile go away.

Seven seconds after the spike, my mind worked on afterburner. I began trying to duck — to make a harsh maneuver in three dimensions, one that would push the F-16 to its formidable limit.

Eight seconds after the spike, a programmed female voice came over my headset with two urgent words: "Counter, counter." My chaff flare system had been tickled to give the added alarm, and I slid my right thumb toward the countermeasures switch on my stick. I wasn't hesitating, but events were out pacing my re-action time.

Nine seconds after the spike, I saw a brilliant red flash to my right; a missile had exploded between my plane and Wilbur's.

We weren't safe yet. SA-6s come packaged in racks of three. Sure enough, Wilbur screamed: *"Missiles in the air!"*

But I never heard Wilbur. Within a second after that red flash, all I could hear was the murderous *bang* that swallowed me whole, like the whale that got Jonah. All I could feel was the biggest jolt of my life. I knew a little some-thing about crashes, but this one took first prize. It was like getting rear-ended by a speeding eighteen-wheeler with an explosive warhead strapped to its hood.

When a plane and missile collide, the plane finishes second.

The SA-6 had scored a face shot. It had soared up from my blind spot and struck my jet square in the belly of its fuselage. For the briefest instant I felt heaved up, as if upper cut by a giant fist, and then I pitched savagely down and to the left. The missile had sheared my plane in two; the nose and cockpit had broken away.

I knew straightaway what had happened. There'd be no more flying of this F-16 — that much was painfully obvious. My console was disintegrating, breaking up before me, twisting and warping like plastic. Fresh from refueling, my plane was a high-altitude gas tank; it had burst into fire. The flames found an eighth-inch space between my oxygen mask and visor. They found the nape of my neck where the left side of my collar had drooped down. There was fire all around me.

I felt the heat and the pain, and for an awful moment I thought my end had come.

So I did what many others have done in desperate situations: I appealed to a force greater than my own. In times of true emergency, you find that your connection opens up real quick — you don't need to dial an access code. *Dear God, please don't let me die now — don't let me die from this.*

All of these events — the bang, the jolt, the pitch, the flames, my prayer — occurred within fractions of a second.

A fraction later I looked down, through the blaze, to the most glorious, blessed sight I'd ever seen: a hard rubber handle, shaped like a snow shovel's, jutting up between my legs. It was a yellow handle, but it shone like gold to me. It bore three words, in white letters on a black background: "PULL TO EJECT."

My next move took no time at all — no more time than it takes a body drowning in adrenaline to pass on a blunt message from the brain.

I reached down with my left hand.

And pulled.

CHAPTER TWO

Jet ejection seats have come a long way since the Vietnam era. In those days, the seats did a great job of springing pilots clear of larger planes like the B-52. But to get that clearance, pilots endured ejection velocities of nearly 60 miles per hour and forces in the 21-G range — high enough to crack a spinal column.

Equally dangerous, an unstable ejection could result in massive flailing injuries to the face and limbs. As a pinwheeling pilot got broadsided by air blasting hundreds of miles per hour, he might easily break an arm, even rip off a leg.

The seat used by the modern U.S. Air Force, McDonnell Douglas's Advanced Concept Ejection Seat, or ACES-II, is a vast improvement. Cast from rigid aluminum alloy, it is a smart seat, with probes and sensors to calculate your airspeed and altitude; it even chooses the point at which your parachute would deploy. An internal gyroscope cuts short any tumble or spin by directing brief thrusts of a tiny rocket motor.

With the ACES-II, your peak acceleration force tops out at ten to twelve Gs, to be withstood for about half a second — generally no problem for a properly seated pilot.

Even so, ejections remain high-risk ventures, for wind can kill. From out of a controlled environment, a person is literally blasted into space. The faster your plane is moving at the point of ejection, the greater the danger — and the progression is lethally exponential. Just two months before, a good friend of mine, an F-15E pilot, found himself flying blind off the Carolina coast when his instruments malfunctioned during a night training flight. A supersonic ejection landed my friend in a wheelchair; his weapon systems officer didn't make it. You can't practice ejections — you study the texts and hope you never have to apply them.

In training we were taught the importance of assuming a good position: both hands on the firing handle; elbows in close, clear of overhanging obstacles; head and neck back, and upper torso erect, to avoid spinal damage from the G-forces; feet extended and thighs flush on the seat. If your legs are raised even an inch or two, the seat's raw force might injure them.

But the fact is, there are two kinds of ejections. There is the kind you have time to prepare for, when you can slow the aircraft and go through your checklist — even do some light housekeeping and secure loose items in the cockpit. And then there is the get-your-butt-out-of-there-yesterday scenario, where you'd better grab that handle fast or something seriously bad is going to happen to you.

They say that pilots have an ingrained reluctance to ditch their planes, but I never hesitated on June 2.

Had I delayed ejecting half a second, I might have been tossed helplessly around the cockpit. I might have spun into G-forces so high that my arms would have stalled of their own weight, too heavy to move. I had no time to adjust my body position. My right hand most likely lingered on the stick, and my neck no doubt angled down as I sought the handle. At liftoff, the seat itself corrected minor posture deviations; the inertia reel straps, linked by rollers to the parachute risers, pulled my shoulders back toward the seat. But even so, my position was less than ideal. I'd just have to take my chances, to play the hand dealt me. To handle whatever came next.

The F-16 is a wonder of futuristic avionics, but the ejection firing handle is an old-fashioned, mechanical device. It's connected to a pulley, with a cable stop at four inches. It takes forty to fifty pounds of force to raise the handle — they don't want you to eject by accident — but it felt like a feather to me, like the sword in the stone. I felt no resistance at all — just a wash of fear and doubt. I hadn't been vaporized in a fireball; God had given me that much. But would the ACES-II leave the aircraft?

What if the seat had been crippled by the warhead? What if the canopy had twisted in its fittings and stuck there, like a swollen wood-framed window? Other jets had canopy breakers — in a pinch you could just smash on through. But the F-16's design prevented you from leaving the plane till the canopy was gone. If the canopy's rocket jettison mechanism failed, you'd have to resort to a series of emergency options.

None of the fallbacks were treats. Their controls ranged along the left side of your seat, from front to rear, and you were to try them in that order. The repercussions got progressively worse as your arm strayed farther past the line for an unimpeded ejection. If the first fallback worked, you'd risk breaking a finger; the next one might lose you that finger; the third could cost you a hand; the fourth might sever your arm.

But those grisly options were moot, since

I had no time to try them. My whole life would depend on my canopy's vanishing act. Either it separated or I was through. *Dear God, please let me out of this plane!*

And so I pulled . . . and heard the instantaneous pop of the jettisoned canopy. Cool air rushed over me. With no elapsed time to speak of, my seat glided up its guide rails and was slung into the air by a rocket catapult.

So far, so good.

As violent as it sounds, the ejection didn't much shake me up; I'd weathered a lot worse when the missile hit. I'd only realize what I'd been through a bit later, when I inventoried my losses to the wind blast. Gone were my visor and a flashlight I'd strapped to my chest. Ripped from my G-suit were the knee boards, plus the camouflage patch with my name and wings. The blast had blown off the patch's facing, cut its stitching like a scissors, while leaving the Velcro pad behind. The heel of my left boot had apparently snagged on something on its way out. Some cobbled nails had stripped loose, exposing the sole's steel plate.

But those were trivial items, to be cataloged after the fact. Now I saw shards of debris around me, pieces of my ruined cockpit, all that was left of a $20-million fighting marvel. It struck me how truly amazing it was that I'd somehow lived to see them.

I'd been reborn in the air — and into a new world of trouble.

The good news was that the SA-6 impact had braked my plane to about 350 miles per hour, moderating the ejection wind blast.

The bad news was that I was five miles high and plunging to the earth and had no idea whether my parachute would work.

Through those first wild microseconds I waited for the pain, for adrenaline to ebb and my body to report the inevitable: that I'd been gravely hurt, that my burning cheeks were just page one. Stunned as I was, I was also calculating how injuries might hinder my evasion and rescue once — and if — I made it to the ground.

My point of view only upped my anxiety. I was falling facedown, my torso parallel to the ground. My eyes were staring at a Bosnian countryside coming at me, as through a slow zoom lens.

Falling and falling, and I knew I'd be conscious to the end.

Of all the ways to die, this would be one of the very bad ones.

At that point, had I gone strictly by the book, I'd have hung tough through four minutes of free fall. I'd have waited for the ACES-II to send up my chute and free me from the seat at a scheduled altitude of 14,000 feet, where the ambient oxygen and temperature were deemed safe to sustain life.

Unfortunately the book didn't cover direct hits by a jumbo fragmentation warhead like the SA-6, which hurled out jagged bits of metal upon impact. Though my seat seemed intact, I couldn't tell what it looked like behind me; I had no way of knowing the condition of the parachute packed inside the headrest. If the parachute canopy itself — twenty-eight stitched panels of wafer-thin, heat-sensitive nylon — had been shredded by shrapnel or wasted by the fire, I'd simply fall to my death, and it wouldn't matter what I did next.

But suppose the parachute deployed only partway. Or suppose the chute itself was fine, but the seat's electronic sequencer — the brain that times the chute's release — was busted. There were backup measures to solve these problems, if need be. But the longer I dallied in free fall, the less time I'd have to be creative.

I wanted to end this harrowing episode — I wanted a chute over my head *now*, thin air notwithstanding. I weighed all the factors as best I could, ten variables at a gulp, my mind racing to beat the band. Within seconds of ejection I decided to *do* something and find out where I stood.

So I took hold of the manual override chute

handle, on the right side of my seat, and drew it back. Straightaway I heard a pop as the little drogue chute whipped out, to help extract the main chute and stabilize my seat. Less than two seconds later I felt a jerk, and then I heard the most wonderful sound, a great billowing, like someone shaking out a gigantic bed sheet. I abruptly found myself descending at a new angle, perpendicular to the ground. The way it was supposed to be.

I couldn't look behind me to see if the chute was full, but I knew I had *something*. I could tell I was falling more slowly; I could hear the nylon canopy rustling in the wind.

To back up for a moment: The reason I couldn't look behind me was that my headrest was in the way; my seat had yet to separate. This confused me for a moment, till I remembered that our ACES-II's manual override handles were in midconversion. With the old model, the one I'd studied during F-16 training at Luke Air Force Base, a short pull of the handle deployed the chute and unlocked the seat at the same time. With the new model, a one-inch pull was enough to ignite a mortar cartridge and launch the parachute. But the lever had to swing an additional six inches to disengage the seat.

I didn't know which model I'd drawn that day. To be honest, I didn't care. The seat made me feel secure, and I was content to ride it, like some stratospheric chairlift, at least for the time being. I'm a pretty aggressive person by nature, but I wasn't inclined to push my luck — I had this image of kicking the seat away and plunging down right behind it. A seated parachute landing would be difficult, if not downright dangerous, but I figured I'd find a way to lose the ACES-II if it didn't release as programmed down the road.

Meanwhile, I had more pressing concerns. With my seared face shrieking for relief, I yanked off my helmet and oxygen mask, disconnected the hose — disabling my seat's backup oxygen tank — and threw the whole assembly earthward. My cheeks promptly felt a little better, but for a moment I wondered how badly my skin was damaged.

Though still fairly high up — the chute released at about 24,000 feet — I felt no signs of hypoxia, no dizziness or tingling. For the first time it occurred to me that my main concerns wouldn't be in the air. They'd be on the ground, on the war-torn land to which I was swirling, ready or not.

I had one big advantage going for me. Unlike most Air Force pilots at Aviano, who'd never been under a parachute, I had ten rides under my belt. I wouldn't panic; I knew what to expect.

My debut had come the summer before my junior year in college, when some friends of mine talked me into jumping at a place in Arizona. After several hours of instruction we went up, and it got real clear to me that leaping out of an airplane was not a rational human act. Though we went out on a static line, which pulled your chute after some seconds of free fall, it felt weird to realize that your existence hinged on two straps between your legs.

That first jump was a total shock to my system. They taught you to scream out your count up to seven, when you'd pull your reserve handle if the static line failed. I stepped clear, into the void — and I was screaming. I *knew* I was screaming, but I couldn't hear my own voice. I'd entered a state of sensory overload; my mind couldn't process what was happening to me.

I was grateful I didn't have *that* to put up with on June 2, 1995.

The following summer I did it the Army way. I was accepted as a ROTC cadet for three weeks of airborne training at Fort Benning, Georgia. This wasn't a career path move — if anything, I might have gotten hurt and risked my future as a pilot. But I loved the adventure of parachuting. By now I was out of shock mode and into controllable anxiety, even if I never felt quite comfortable in that harness. I loved testing myself, to see how I'd perform in a pinch.

Those are the times we get to know ourselves best.

I had ample time over Bosnia to use my airborne training. By skipping free fall and pulling the chute early, I'd slowed my average rate of descent to 12 miles per hour, effectively doubling the length of my ride. It would be twenty-five minutes or more before I'd touch down.

No sooner had the chute deployed than I was buffeted by high-altitude gusts, wafted sideways as much as down. The little drogue chute was flitting everywhere, like some crazy kite. What if it got snarled in the big chute? In every single one of my ten practice chute rides, some small problem had cropped up. I wondered what was behind and above me now, when I most needed a sure, safe trip. Had the missile punched holes in the nylon? Were my risers twisted? Had one of the lines settled atop the canopy, blocking its full inflation?

None of these conditions were necessarily perilous. But in the worst case, my descent could accelerate; if I came down too fast, all the training in the world might not be enough. And I knew too well that the prospects were bleak for evaders with broken legs.

I went to work, performing the mental equipment check drilled into me at Fort Benning and reinforced at survival school at Fairchild Air Force Base in Spokane. There was a strict order: canopy, visor, mask, life preserver, survival seat kit, four-line release. By now, however, my visor and mask were gone. I couldn't see my canopy, and the seat prevented me from reaching my four-line release, the parachute's steering mechanism. The life preserver, a horse collar that inflated automatically upon contact with salt water, was a nonplayer. So the check wasn't all that useful, but I ran it through a dozen times or more. It was something familiar I could cling to, a reminder that I'd been trained for just this kind of contingency.

Then I heard the throaty roar of a jet, off in the clouds above me: Wilbur! I reached down to the left of the ejection handle, at the front edge of my seat pan, and found the toggle switch to send a distress signal over the Guard channel. When set in the on position, the switch automatically activated a radio beacon — a high-pitched burst — at the time of seat/man separation.

Choosing a switch position was a matter of pilot preference; heading into Deny Flight sorties, I'd always left the beacon off. It seemed logical that I wouldn't want to hang a neon sign over my head as I drifted through the air after a shootdown.

Now, in the crunch, security counted less than making contact. The military had two firm prerequisites for launching a rescue effort. They had to make certain the evader was alive, and they needed to confirm his position within one nautical mile.

As of now, I was batting 0 for 2.

I took the gamble. I switched on the beacon for three seconds, then turned it off again, fearful of detection by hostile forces. In a normal ejection, I knew the beacon wouldn't transmit before seat/man separation. But in this unusual case, with my parachute deployed and me still in the seat, I thought I might as well take a shot.

Seconds later the jet noise faded off to the southwest. I knew Wilbur would stay up there in a rescue cap as long as he could. When a flight lead came home without his wing-man, it was like leaving a part of himself out there. But I also knew that Wilbur couldn't circle forever — he'd have to be mindful of a follow-up assault, and he'd be all the more vulnerable without a wingman to watch his back.

I tried another tack, reaching into my survival vest pocket for my handheld radio, which could also emit a beacon. But the radio was taped and sealed inside two heavy ziplock bags, as protection for watery landings, and I wasn't willing to rip them open at 20,000 feet. If I dropped the radio, I was out of luck. I'd wait to communicate on the ground.

Given the cloud cover, I assumed that Wilbur had no way of seeing I'd successfully ejected. As far as NATO knew, I was unaccounted for, and there was nothing more I could do about it.

After another equipment check, I looked down and saw the city of Bosanski Petrovac a few miles to my west and a highway to the southeast. Beyond the road, farther south, I could make out a plume of black smoke and what looked like a brushfire — the crash point of my plane's fuselage. The whole scene seemed terribly surreal to me. Just minutes before, I'd been at the command of my F-16, on a routine mission, wholly in control. A few hours before that, I'd left the tranquil village I called home. Now I hung between sky and ground, helpless and alone.

Was this really happening?

I didn't hesitate to answer, to mentally slap myself: *Better get your act in gear.* The facts weren't pretty, but they were plain. I was over hostile territory, and it was my job to evade all comers until I could be rescued. The planning, the mind-set, the will to do that job, had to take root here and now. There was no time for wishful thinking. I had business to attend to.

Canopy, visor, mask, life preserver, survival seat kit, four-line release . . .

At 14,000 feet the ACES-II dropped away from me as advertised. Though it had served me well, I was glad to be rid of it. As the seat fell, my seat kit, the pillow-sized shell still clipped to my hips, released a twenty-five-foot nylon cord. My vinyl rucksack hung at the bottom; the size of a briefcase, it contained much of my essential survival gear. Halfway up the line dangled a one-man rubber life raft, now partially inflated. At the top, still attached to my seat kit, was the compact hit-and-run kit with my auxiliary gear. When the wind caught my hanging cargo and blew me in widening circles, I wound the line twice around my leg, to draw the raft closer and reduce the oscillation.

With the seat back no longer blocking me, I could finally inspect my parachute canopy. For the first time in my life, it was perfect. Each of its panels — dyed orange, white, green, or brown — looked factory-fresh.

Ever since I'd ejected, I'd seen clouds in all directions — except for the cylinder of crisp blue sky right around me. I was in the hole of the doughnut, the last place I wanted to be. I could see the ground clearly in the afternoon light and knew I'd reached the level where I could be seen as well.

While I was now well past the city, the highway worried me. It was an east-west road, but the stretch I was nearing curved north-south. As a hard surface with steady traffic — I spied a large truck inching along — that highway would be the worst place imaginable to land. Most of its near environs weren't much better. To the north stretched flat, brown croplands, sitting-duck territory; to the immediate south and east, a scattering of farmhouses and open pastures.

My best bet seemed to lie farther south, in a dense wood that rose into a big hill — the kind of remote high ground well suited to evasion and radio communication. True, I might snag on a tree and get injured or delayed, but a little luck and some inspired steering should get me to a patch of ground, with a shot at some decent concealment. I needed to veer south.

I addressed my four-line release, a pair of red lanyard handles above either side of my head. A tug on both of them would release four panels at the rear of the chute's canopy; those panels would bulge out, as air moving through the parachute escaped at the point of least resistance. The end results: I'd be pro-

pelled forward, the best way to land, and I'd
be able to steer around rocks or power lines
with subsequent tugs on either handle.

But as I grabbed for the lanyards, I came
a cropper: the right handle had spooled up
into a rear riser's sleeve, out of reach. I pulled
hard on a front riser directly, to see if I might
steer the thing that way, but it barely budged.
I tried three or four more times: no dice.

I was at the mercy of the wind.

The truck had stopped, not far in front of
me. It looked like a military truck with a canvas top in back, the type seen on *Hogan's Heroes*. The type they crammed with soldiers.

With a rising urgency, I performed one last
equipment check, then did the same for my
body. My fingers and toes were all accounted
for. The burns had leveled off into a chronic
but bearable smarting. I was more worried
about my back, after the extreme G-forces of
ejection. It felt okay, but I wouldn't know for
sure till my feet hit the ground.

Still high above the ground, I was passing
over the highway when a car joined the truck
on the road's shoulder. The wind was ruthless,
pushing me on to the southeast. Under my
candy-colored, twenty-eight-foot canopy, I
was as conspicuous as the Goodyear blimp.
I could almost feel the sets of eager eyes boring
in at me.

63

Was I a curiosity? A target? A hostage-to-be?

I recalled what I'd been told, many times, by the intel people back in Aviano: there were no friendly forces in Bosnia, no safe areas, no one you could count on. This was not World War II, when front lines meant something and the French Resistance harbored many an American pilot. This was modern warfare, where it seemed that the only thing uniting a crazy quilt of factions was a shared distrust of the U.N. peacekeepers and the NATO air-power behind them.

I'd lost count of the prayers I'd recited since my plane was hit, since that awful jolt that seemed so long ago. I'd prayed that I'd survive the missile's impact and the flames that had enveloped me; that the bubble canopy would release, allowing a safe ejection; that my seat would function and send up a working chute.

I'd been delivered all I'd asked for, and now I was asking for more. *Dear God, let me land in a safe place, without harm.*

And down by that menacing highway, they sat there waiting for me, watching and waiting for their package to arrive.

CHAPTER THREE

I was six years old when I fell in love with the sky.

We were living in Long Beach, California, where my father got his private pilot's license while serving at the naval hospital there. As the oldest of three children, I always looked forward to going out alone with Dad. In February 1972 he took me up in a Cessna 150, a little red and white two-seater, and we flew out to Catalina Island, thirty-five minutes each way.

It was one of those brilliant winter days in southern California, when the sea and sky are flawless and the world seems Crayola blue. The trip bewitched me. I was seized by the easy speed of it, by the eagle's-eye view. Disneyland and Knott's Berry Farm were terrific, all right, but that Cessna was the ride to end all.

I still have the certificate from the Catalina control tower, signed in my neatest first-grade hand: "This is to certify that Scott O'Grady has navigated the airways and flown up to Santa Catalina's unique Airport in the Sky, which overlooks the ocean from an altitude of 1,602 feet."

When we were little, my sister, Stacy, and my brother, Paul, and I could be terrors. One baby-sitter was so traumatized that she fled the house, wouldn't even come back to get paid. We were definitely daredevils at heart. When my father took us to the Cyclone, the famous old roller coaster in Coney Island, we rode it a dozen times before consenting to leave.

Through my boyhood I had the usual obsessions: swashbuckling pirates, Wyatt Earp, *The Lord of the Rings.* At eleven I became infatuated with all things ninja, down to a pair of black slippers I wore into the ground. I begged my parents to let me move to Atlanta, to apprentice to a martial arts instructor I'd read about.

By the eighth grade came a new fixation: I was going to be a pilot, end of discussion. Actually it was more specific than that: I wanted to be a fighter pilot in the U.S. Air Force. The basic excitement of aviation — of going faster than people had a right to, of being in the *air* — was a powerful lure. So was my fascination with World War II aces like Pappy Boyington; I'd be moored to our TV set whenever *Baa Baa Black Sheep* came on the air.

But I longed for more than simple adventure, or to fly the most advanced aircraft; I wanted a life with purpose. To serve in the U.S. Air Force was to serve the best country in the world. I guess I'm old-fashioned that way; I genuinely get goose bumps when the national anthem is played at a ball game.

We grew up in a patriotic family. My mother hung the flag at the front of our house each morning — as soon as it grew the least bit tattered, she'd run out a new one. My father went through Officer Candidate School in the Marine Corps; he later volunteered for Vietnam during his hitch in the Navy and briefly headed up a surgical team off the coast there. (Much later he switched gears to become a radiologist.) I missed my dad terribly during his three months at sea, but I also remember how proud I was to see him come home in a uniform.

My parents, of course, were products of their own upbringing and family history. My grandmother O'Grady came over from Ireland in steerage; she worked as a maid before she married my grandfather, a New York City policeman. On my mother's side, my grandfather Giustra was the son of a widowed seamstress and the oldest of five children. The family breadwinner at the age of twelve, Frank Giustra eventually put himself through college and medical school and later became one of Brooklyn's first pediatric cardiologists. He also raised nine children with my grandmother, a generation that produced two doctors, two teachers, an engineer, and three business professionals.

As my immediate family moved — from New York to Long Beach to New Jersey to Spokane — I crisscrossed the nation by car and witnessed just how great it was. My dad would route us through places rich in history; I got to see Gettysburg and Manassas, Plymouth and Jamestown, Mount Rushmore and Custer's Last Stand. Later on, I'd have the same sense of awe when I first saw the Capitol or the White House — I'd think of the giants who'd worked and strived there, and I'd be humbled.

I get the same feelings today when I visit the Vietnam Veterans Memorial in Washington, D.C. I like to start at the edge of it, where people are whispering, then move slowly in. The crowd quiets, until at the center it is deadly silent; that just touches my heart.

As a boy, my favorite presidents were Andrew Jackson, a general as well as a statesman, and Abraham Lincoln, for the values he stood for. Lincoln seemed like such a large and powerful man, yet somehow gentle at the same time. He didn't have to throw his weight around — he prevailed through spiritual force.

I understood early on that this country was founded by people who'd left their native lands to search for personal and religious freedom. And that it was preserved by the citizen soldier, the common person who stood ready to answer any threat.

Nine years after the trip to Catalina, after the family had moved to Spokane, Washington, Dad and I went up again. We flew out to Kalispell, Montana, and at some point over the Cabinet Mountains my dad surprised me. He gave me the yoke.

Now, *that* was a charge. I didn't have to maneuver, just held the throttle steady. But it was quite a challenge to keep the Cessna moving straight, to keep track of altitude and heading and airspeed all at the same time. I quickly discovered that you flew more smoothly with a light, fingertip touch on the stick — a plane wasn't something to manhandle.

For the two or three minutes I held that yoke, I felt a new freedom. I was fifteen, when every rule and boundary offended me, and suddenly I had room to move in three dimensions; I was steering a machine two miles up in the air.

It seemed remarkable that you could do this and get *paid* for it. Not long after that, I began working toward my own pilot's license. Flying was more than a hobby for me, even then. It was my future, my calling.

In Spokane I was your typical clean-cut teenager, never in any real trouble, but I did have a little mischievous streak. After skiing, my favorite winter sport was to take the family's Chevy Suburban to Manito Park at night. With brother Paul and some friends at my side, I'd rev that wagon up and charge full tilt for a sledding hill. On a good night we'd hit 50 miles per hour on the way down. And if we hit a bump just right, I could get that Suburban airborne.

My parents never pushed me along any particular path. I could be anything I wanted, as long as I had fun and did it well. I learned early in life to set my own goals, then figure out how to reach them. I wasn't one of those golden boys; few things came easily to me. But I wasn't afraid to work hard until I found my niche. And I hated to lose, or be passed over — stubbornness maybe the leading O'Grady trait.

My sports career was a case in point. My

best sport was skiing, where I wasn't checked by caution; I liked pushing the envelope, going as fast as I could. Despite average foot speed, I also held my own in soccer — I had a knack for anticipating how a play would unfold.

But at Lewis & Clark High School in Spokane, only one sport really mattered: varsity football, where the cool guys made their mark. Unfortunately I entered my junior year at 125 pounds; I was the lightest kid going out for the team. With no future at linebacker, I set my sights on placekicking. I'd just learn how to do it, score a bushel of points, and watch my status soar.

It was probably the dumbest idea I ever had in my life.

I got help from a guy named Jim Gaetano, who'd been a kicker on his college team a few years before. We practiced hard at it, two and three hours after school, kick after kick after kick. I got pretty good and was aching to prove myself, but I couldn't get into a game. The coach didn't have a regular kicker — he rotated among several players — but he never called my name.

Meanwhile, I was getting creamed at the scrimmages, where they'd pit all the scrawny weaklings against the starters. I played wide receiver — and sacrificial lamb. One time I got hit and woke up ten yards later.

Toward the end of the season, Lewis & Clark took on its archrival, Gonzaga Prep. Our team's high point came when one of our guys intercepted a pass and ran it back for a touchdown. I was cheering on the bench, minding my own business, when I heard the coach growl: "O'Grady, get in there, and go kick the extra point."

Holy smokes. I couldn't believe it. Here was the chance I'd been craving, and now, with no notice, they were throwing me into the fray. I was totally unprepared; I was in a daze.

A placekicker needs to move forward as the ball is hiked, so he can meet it at the tee. If you wait till the ball gets there, it's too late; your kick will get blocked by the opposing team.

Which is exactly what happened. I hesitated, they rushed, and the ball and I were smothered. After waiting all year long to kick, I'd flubbed my big shot. In my disgust, I threw myself into a half-flip, half-somersault — and landed flat on my back, like Charlie Brown after Lucy swipes the ball away.

Later on I heard that our coaching staff kept rewinding the game tape to the point of my flip. They thought it was hilarious; it was the sole bright spot in a losing effort. They watched it about ten times.

I never left the bench after that; my gridiron exploits were over.

My interest in flying became more than theoretical the following summer, when I started working toward my private pilot's license out of Felts Field in Spokane. I learned all the basics: how to control an aircraft's pitch up and down, to roll left and right with the ailerons, to "trim" the plane and keep it level.

I wouldn't say I was a natural. As with everything else, I gradually picked things up, learned from my mistakes, figured out what worked for me. After a dozen accompanied flights, I was declared ready for my first solo. The instructor went up with me at first to fly around for a while. Once he thought I had things under control, we landed and he hopped out of the Cessna.

At first everything was fine. I focused on my procedures: talking on the radio, handling the throttle and the flaps, flying the proper box pattern. I did my first "touch-and-go," where the landing gear glances off the ground and you take right off again: perfect. Moving downwind and parallel to the runway, I was heading into my second touch-and-go, to be followed by another box and a full stop. Strictly routine.

My mother once said that her first solo flight was the second biggest thrill of her life —

right after giving birth to her children. I'd been pretty calm to that point, but then I made a big mistake: I looked over to the instructor's seat.

There was nobody there. I'd been too busy to think about it, but now it hit me: I was by myself. This wasn't Knott's Berry Farm. I was going 90 miles an hour, flying 1,000 feet up — not very big numbers, but adequate to rearrange my vertebrae.

I got a dose of the willies. When I came down, I pulled back a hair too much on the yoke, ballooned two feet off the runway, hit hard enough to bounce off a second time, and landed roughly once more. "I'm going to make this one my full stop," I informed the control tower. Knowing how nervous I was, he said only one word: "Congratulations."

It was enough to make you glad that men didn't have babies.

In the fall of my senior year, having slaved to boost my grades, I applied for admission to the Air Force Academy in Colorado Springs. It sounded like a dream school. The campus, the facilities, the education — all were first-rate. I was about to be nominated by my congressman, Tom Foley, and my grades were fine. But the verbal score on my SAT exam fell short of the Academy's standard.

The standard wasn't flexible. I was rejected.

That was a blow to my ego, no question, a serious disappointment. But I didn't let myself get discouraged or sit there and cry. My long-term objective, after all, wasn't the Academy. My goal was to become a fighter pilot, regardless of any detours along the way. I could still enroll in a college ROTC program and get my wings. When one door shut, you found another. You moved on.

For the next year and change I drifted through the University of Washington in Seattle. I switched my major from aeronautical engineering to accounting to business to forestry. I joined a big fraternity and partied hearty — that was a lot of fun, even if my frat brothers considered ROTC a geeky thing to do. After taking the winter quarter off to ski and wash dishes in Sun Valley, Idaho, I came back to Seattle, where I lived with my dad. Pretty soon he'd figured out that I'd stopped going to class.

"What do you want to do?" my father asked me.

"I want to fly," I said.

As usual, he had an idea. A friend of his had a brother attending Embry-Riddle Aeronautical University in Florida, and gave the school good reviews. It sounded fine to me.

I could fly, get my degree, and live in Daytona Beach — *outstanding*.

I applied and was accepted for the fall term in 1986. But there was a hitch: the Daytona Beach campus was full up. I was invited to enroll at a satellite campus, instead . . . in Prescott, Arizona.

The location didn't look too promising on my map. It looked even worse after I boarded a little puddle jumper out of Phoenix for the last eighty miles to Prescott. I was used to the green forests and mountains of Washington State; on a sunny day at my campus in Seattle, you could see Mount Rainier. But the farther we got from Phoenix and its backyard swimming pools, the more the landscape mimicked the face of the moon. As we descended into Prescott, I looked in vain for the campus; all I could see was bare ground and desolation. *Jiminy Cricket,* I thought, *what am I getting myself into?*

An old, rickety school bus was there to pick me up, along with a few other students, and then it lurched off into the arid heat. My lodgings were at a downtown hotel — the school overbooked its dorms, to compensate for students who'd get depressed and drop out — but I decided to check in first on campus. The bus creaked up a hill and stopped at a small cluster of two-story apartment buildings, by some bushes that wanted to be trees but couldn't get that far. Then it swung into town, where the other students got off. We were headed back out, just me and the driver, when I asked him where the school was.

"Oh, that was back at the first stop," he said.

"Oh, my God," I said. Those two-story buildings were dormitories. The academic buildings were nearby, down a slight incline, and easy to miss; they were only *one* story high, and painted brown to blend into the scenery.

Once I recovered from culture shock, Prescott grew on me. True, the social scene wasn't much beyond the Fourth of July rodeo. There was about one woman at Embry-Riddle for every twenty men — if a girl showed her face on campus, she'd have a boyfriend the next day.

But I had plenty to do without distractions. I was aiming at a B.S. in aeronautical science, which featured courses in physics, chemistry, calculus, meteorology, and engineering. I studied hard; mediocre academics could capsize my master plan. Plus I put a lot of time into ROTC and eventually rose to vice commander of a corps of more than a hundred cadets.

In the summer after my sophomore year,

I underwent four weeks of field training at Lowry Air Force Base in Denver. It was my first taste of real military life, drill instructor and all, and I was amazed at how much activity they packed into a fourteen-hour day. The highlight was a two-day stint in the woods with a survival instructor, the first person I ever saw eat an ant. As the insect du jour was optional, I begged off.

Before my junior year began, I won a rare pilot scholarship from the Air Force, which covered the costs of my last two years of college. I also signed the required long-term contract with the military. I thought it was a pretty good deal: they agreed to teach me to be a pilot, and I agreed to spend the next nine years flying for them.

Meanwhile, I was piling up flight ratings — nine of them by the time I left Embry-Riddle, from seaplane to commercial multi-engine to certified flight instructor. I even earned my rating for gliders, a unique airborne sensation — freer and more natural on the one hand, more restricted on the other. Your glider could stay out there indefinitely, as long as you found lift from thermals or air currents. But when the lift ran out, you didn't have a vote on when you landed.

I knew that these credentials might help boost me into a top pilot training program, but that wasn't why I earned them. Each rating was a quest for me, a new way of exploring an old thrill.

Looking back on it, Embry-Riddle might have been the best thing that could have happened to me. The Air Force Academy is a spectacular place; of all my friends who've gone there, none regret it. But you get a different kind of growing experience outside a military environment. You learn to live on your own, take care of yourself, and interact with all kinds of people. I became a self-reliant person in Prescott, a quality I'd need for the rigors to come.

The night before our graduation, I begged off on meeting my family for dinner. I had one piece of unfinished business: a professor had volunteered to raise a grade if I rewrote a paper. I stayed up late to complete the job, and when I walked up to get my diploma the next day, they added two words to my name: *cum laude.*

I had my degree. I'd earned my commission as a second lieutenant in the Air Force. Best of all, I'd been accepted into the Euro-NATO Joint Jet Pilot Training Program, at Sheppard Air Force Base in Texas — my first choice, the best possible springboard to my goal.

Highly competitive in its admissions, the

Euro-NATO program was unlike any other. When we assembled in November 1989, most of my forty-two classmates hailed from other NATO countries, primarily Holland and Germany; my best friend there would be a guy from Belgium named Pierre De Nys. Our instructors came from places like Italy and Canada and Denmark, and most had fighter experience, which was unusual of itself. As they didn't use simulators at Euro-NATO, we got more flying time and check rides than the norm. It wasn't rare to go up five times a week — I was in heaven.

There was more pressure here as well. In other programs a student who wasn't quite up to speed could move into larger, multiseat aircraft, tankers or transporters. But at Euro-NATO you graduated to become a fighter pilot or not at all. If you stumbled — if you missed even a few days' flying with the flu — you might be moved back to the next incoming class. If you couldn't handle the curriculum, you washed out.

It was an incredibly demanding year — we should all have gotten master's degrees. Each semester began with a block of academics: courses in navigation and meteorology and formation flying; link trainers for bad-weather practice at a stationary instrument console; instructional tapes and stacks of books to cart home each night.

Every morning, as early as five o'clock, we'd start the day with a full-class assembly. After a few words from the flight commander, the unit safety monitor would give a "stand-up" quiz on some emergency procedure. He'd lay out a scenario and call on a student at random, who'd stand up to address the problem. If the monitor didn't like what he was hearing, he'd move to someone else; there were mornings when four or five people would be standing there till someone solved the puzzle.

The made-up emergency might involve engine or instrument failure, or a landing gear problem, or some glitch in the oxygen system. But no matter what it was, you always began your answer with a standard checklist: "Sir, the first thing I would do is maintain aircraft control, analyze the situation, take appropriate action, and land as soon as conditions permit." Then you'd consider what was wrong and what help you might enlist on the ground or in the air.

For our very first quiz as a class, the scenario dealt with a student's first ride in a T-37, our basic training jet; the hypothetical plane had gone out of control during a practice maneuver. "Okay, Russell," the monitor said in his thick Italian accent, "whatcha gonna do?"

Russell was from Florida, a great guy. He

recited the checklist and then he asked, "Sir, I understand this is my first ride in a T-37?"

"Yes, that's right," the monitor said.

"So I am with a flight instructor?"

"Yes, that's right."

And Russell said, "Well, sir, I turn to the instructor and say, 'You have the jet!' "

The students burst out laughing, but our instructors didn't think it was too funny. As for Russell, he decided that pilot training wasn't for him.

We trained on the T-37 for the first half of that year, flying more intensively as the semester wore on. Though essentially a Cessna with jet engines, by no means high-performance, it was nonetheless a giant step up from a propeller-driven aircraft. Rather than go up in a T-shirt and jeans, with your sunglasses and headset, you now wore a flightsuit and G-suit, and a parachute as well. You'd put on your helmet and oxygen mask — and at that point you'd be suffocating in the humidity of Wichita Falls.

In contrast to the Cessna's yoke-type steering column, the T-37 had a control stick between your legs and a throttle at your left. There was a new array of instruments to master, gauges for engine speed, exhaust gas, and so on. The trainer plane *sounded* different; it whined rather than whirred. It also moved a lot faster than anything I'd ever flown before, with a top speed exceeding 250 miles per hour.

More speed spelled more risk. One day, my friend Pierre flew the wrong pattern and climbed into my flight path. He never saw me — if I hadn't dodged, we'd have crashed in the air. (I never missed a chance to harass him about it later: "Remember that time you almost killed me?")

The T-37 was a side-by-side two-seater, for student and instructor, but you advanced rapidly to solo. After taking a plane up alone for the first time, tradition demanded that you be dunked in a pool of dirty water outside the pilot training building. Summer or winter, it didn't matter — if the pool's surface froze, they'd just smash the ice before slinging you in there.

In our second semester we moved on to the T-38. This little plane was a record-breaker in its time, a high-performance jet with a rocket motor, complete with afterburner. For the students it was a whole new ball game, and it would take a while before we could hold our own.

When you're on top of your game as a pilot, you feel like you're "ahead" of the airplane; you're making all the right moves before the situation demands them. But when I first took control of a T-38 and pushed it past 300 miles per hour, it threw me for a loop. The sensation wasn't one of blinding speed, but rather of events streaking at you too quickly for your mind to react. And once you got behind, it could snowball, like an assembly line gone haywire — till you hung on for dear life to the tail of the plane, straining to drag yourself back into the cockpit to regain control.

I learned fast on the T-38 — I had no choice. I got used to the pacing, the quick shifts in altitude. I came to anticipate the radio calls I'd need for clearances on departure routing. Gradually I drew even with the plane, then ahead of it, but my first solo was still a kick in the cranium. I felt like a rocket was strapped to my back.

A few months before the end of our year, it fell time to declare our preference for the jet we hoped to fly in the military. I knew I wanted a single-seat plane; as a pilot I hankered for total accountability and control. Beyond that, I was hopelessly uncertain — I just couldn't decide between the F-15C Eagle and the F-16 Viper. I liked the F-15 because its mission lay exclusively in air-to-air combat, which seemed most exciting to me. The F-16 was a dual-role aircraft: it fought both air-to-air and air-to-ground, although the latter — dropping bombs — was primary.

On the flip side, I preferred the F-16 as an *airplane*. I'd long been infatuated with single-seat, single-engine aircraft: the P-51 from World War II, the F-86 from the Korean conflict. The F-16 upheld that tradition, while the F-15 was a dual-engine plane. You couldn't say one was better; it was like Corvettes and Ferraris, a question of style more than function. (Another Air Force fighter, the A-10 Warthog, was my third pick. A dual-engine, air-to-ground attack plane, its air-to-air mission was limited to self-defense.)

After going back and forth about fifty times a day, I finally placed the F-15C first on my written wish list, and the F-16 second.

And a few weeks later I changed my mind.

The turning point was my first low-level flight in a T-38. At just 500 feet above the surface, with ground objects whizzing past, the sensation of speed was fantastic — far more intense than even a supersonic flight at five miles up. It got me thinking. If I flew the F-15, I might never get the chance to fly so low — there wouldn't be much call for it within an air-to-air mission.

When the exercise was over, I sat down with my Norwegian instructor, a former F-16 pilot; he, too, was captivated by low-level flying. As I talked things over with him and other F-16 veterans, I saw the air-to-ground mission in a new light.

Consider, to begin with, that the only way to win a war was to place an eighteen-year-old infantryman and his rifle on enemy soil. Next, you had to support that soldier by putting bombs on tactical and strategic targets — by using planes that "hauled iron." The F-16 and A-10, then, were at the tip of the Air Force spear. Air-to-air specialists like the F-15 were vital, but as a *support* asset. They took out threats that enabled *other* planes to deliver their ordnance.

In football terms, the F-16 would be the running back, carrying the ball to pay dirt; the F-15 was the offensive lineman who buried would-be tacklers.

You needed both players, but only one of them could score.

As I spent more time with those former F-16 pilots, I was struck by their attitude and personal style. Within the universe of fighter aircraft, you'd find that a plane's mission drove the personality of the men inside it. There was a definite mentality among the A-10 pilots: rugged, down-and-dirty, indifferent to glory — well grounded, if you will. They were Warthogs and proud of it. They even seemed to be *built* the same: short and stocky, like fireplugs.

At the other pole, F-15 pilots were the ultimate masters of the sky, the elite of the elite, heirs to the Red Baron's glamour. Their work was highly technical and unforgiving; small mistakes could cost lives. Every fighter pilot strove for perfection, but the F-15 guys made a religion of it.

At some neighborhood in between you'd find the F-16 community — and the more I got to know it, the more I wanted to put up stakes there. The pilots were professional yet friendly, hardworking but quick to joke. Most of all, they were deeply fraternal; they genuinely cared about one another.

I knew I could be happy in an F-15; it's a fabulous plane, no question about it. But I also hoped that the luck of the draw might favor me and that I'd get the *second* pick on my wish list.

It all came to a head on Assignment Night in November 1990, when we'd learn which jet was in our future. A new pilot's assignment depended, first of all, on the needs of the Air Force and what planes were available. In a down year — after an appropriations cutback, for example — you could excel throughout your training and still get packed off to a desk job.

Once the "drop" — the set of planes reserved for a class — was determined, student preferences were considered in order of class ranking. You were judged as a whole person — for your pilot skills first, but also for academics, professionalism, and military bearing. The student ranked at the top would generally get his first pick; the one ranked at the bottom would take whatever was left over.

Timing was everything, as the drop varied wildly from class to class. There were more F-16s in the Air Force than any other fighter, but that was no guarantee I'd get one — even if the F-15, my first choice, was unavailable to me.

There were certain planes I knew I *didn't* want, like the F-111, an older model being phased out, and the RF-4, which did only reconnaissance. I also knew that at least two of the thirteen American graduates in my class would be selected to stay on at Sheppard as instructor pilots, one each for the T-37 and T-38. That assignment was by no means an insult — those chosen would be higher-ranked pilots with good personalities for teaching. But it wasn't how I wanted to start my Air Force career.

As we trooped into the officers' club for our ceremony, we were all on edge. Assignment Night was structured for maximum suspense; heading into it, we knew neither our individual rankings nor the makeup of our drop. And we wouldn't be called in any particular order — you just had no clue what was coming.

Our class had rigged up an elaborate, carnival-style construction, with a large frame holding two rows of wooden plane silhouettes, one for each type of jet in the NATO forces. After your name was called, and an instructor introduced you with some funny story, you'd stand about eight feet away and throw a beanbag at the plane you hoped to get. If the silhouette toppled and nothing else happened, you'd throw again.

But when you struck the plane you'd been assigned to, all heck broke loose. An electronic buzzer sounded, a siren light took to spinning, and an overhead projector flashed two photos: a picture of your future plane, then one of you — helmet in hand, the hero pose — by your T-38. Everyone would go nuts. Your fellow students would dogpile you, smacking you in the head, shrieking like banshees — it was total frenzy.

I was one of the last to be called. It didn't look good for my F-16; five or six of the Americans had already gotten one. I hoped for the best, took the beanbag and a deep breath. I tossed it straight at the F-16 silhouette: direct hit.

The buzzer sounded.

The light flashed.

Two seconds later, I was thrashing about under a pile of wild and crazy lieutenants and screaming louder than any of them. It was such a choice moment in my life. I'd been dreaming of it since the eighth grade and pushing toward it for four years without a break. No, it hadn't come easy, but I knew then that all my work had been worthwhile.

The Americans in my class had been favored with an incredibly good drop: seven F-16s, two F-15Es (a two-seater version), and two A-10s, in addition to the instructor planes. I'd lucked out; there'd been no F-15Cs on tap.

A month later, at graduation, our wings were pinned to our chests. We were U.S. Air Force pilots for real now.

It was time to start learning how to fight.

CHAPTER FOUR

Before assuming the controls of an F-16, I had one more bridge to cross, a last stepping-stone: a basic fighter training course at Holloman Air Force Base in Alamogordo, New Mexico.

At Holloman our perspective took a quantum shift. Flying, of itself, was no longer the issue; the basics of navigation or aerobatics were well under our belts. Now we'd employ our plane not as merely a flying machine, but a *fighting* machine — an airborne platform for delivering weapons. We'd learn basic fighter maneuvers and formations, contracts and tactics, and since the F-16 had a dual role, I'd be learning them for both air-to-air and air-to-ground missions.

To ease our transition, we'd be working out of an AT-38 — a plane identical to our old friend the T-38, except for being painted in two shades of camouflage blue. We called it the Smurf Jet.

Air-to-air flying is fluid and dynamic; you're maneuvering against a moving target that is doing the same against you. In the World War II, whites-of-their-eyes era, the top flying aces were tremendous stylists, known for signature moves. Today, with the vast advances in aviation technology, we rely more on proven principles. Our basic maneuvers are universal. Even so, a creative pilot can still carve out an advantage; you might say that air-to-air combat has become a super-technical art form.

A pilot's technique is defined by his purpose. There are defensive missions, where you maintain a cap over a home airfield against incoming planes. Then there are offensive counterair missions, where a fighter seeks out enemy aircraft, airfields, or SAM sites for the kill.

Whether on offense or defense, you must also consider how the sides are drawn. In a typical air combat maneuver, with two planes against two, teamwork is primary; a flight lead and wingman must back each other up, help each other out of jams, coordinate their attacks. Once they get into a two-on-one scenario, they may close in to checkmate the remaining enemy — all the while taking care not to get bitten.

At Holloman, everyone's favorite training

exercise was the dogfight: one against one, in close and visual, like a knife fight in a phone booth. Though the AT-38s carried no weapons or simulated displays, we maneuvered just as we would in combat. Sometimes you'd start with a plane at eleven or one o'clock, right in front of you — that's when you'd go on the offensive. When the other guy was at your six o'clock, you'd try to shift to a less vulnerable position. And when your opponent was at three or nine o'clock, the scenario was neutral, and both sides would scramble for an edge.

In a dogfight you needed to grasp the laws of physics and apply them to your aircraft. Each action had a trade-off. The more tightly you turned, for example, the more airspeed and energy you'd lose in the process, which meant that your next turn would be that much lazier. It wasn't enough to know your own plane's capabilities; you also needed a working knowledge of your adversary's tactics and weapons.

And there was one more dimension for the fighter pilot to deal with, beyond science and art and technical mastery: the physiological stresses on his body. Hard maneuvering injected him into a high-gravitational environment. He'd need to counter those stresses to function and to survive.

When you sit in a chair — or fly in a straight line — you are pulling one G, normal earth gravity. A really good roller coaster can get you as high as three Gs at the bottom of its plunge. Once you exceed five Gs, you are at risk of passing out; the forces pool your blood away from the brain to the lowest parts of your body.

The problem is that an F-16 pilot can encounter as much as nine Gs — the maximum for any modern fighter — when pulling out of a steep dive or making a sharp turn. The bladdered G-suit helps to compensate, but not nearly enough. To raise your blood pressure and squeeze a sufficient blood supply back up to your head, you need to strain and constrict your muscles, especially in your lower body. At the same time, you have to keep breathing — which isn't so easy with nine Gs compressing your chest cavity. At Holloman we learned how to do it: a hard, deep inhale, held for three seconds, and then a quick, rough exhale.

We practiced our straining techniques in a centrifuge tuned to the G-force profile of each pilot's future plane. As long as I kept my head still while sitting in the closed compartment, I had no dizziness or sensation of spinning. But the centrifuge was tough to go through, nonetheless; at nine Gs, I was carrying 1,350 pounds. I could feel my face sag, my eyes droop. When I got out, I had a temporary case of freckles: tiny capillaries had burst all over my face, arms, and legs.

High-G training could spoil you for more ordinary fun. Just before I finished up at Euro-NATO, I spent a day at Six Flags in Dallas with a classmate, Lance Glidden. We'd both grown up as roller-coaster nuts — the kind of kids who'd raise their hands and scream — and we tried the biggest coasters there.

But two or three Gs didn't cut it anymore. We were bored. We'd found a bigger, higher, wilder ride — and it was about to get wilder still.

If air-to-air combat was a warp-speed chess match, air-to-ground was a three-dimensional math problem. Though your target was fixed, it was no simple feat to drop a bomb at the precise release point. The window of opportunity was narrow — a few seconds or less — and the variables many. What was your plane's altitude, attitude, and airspeed? Were you climbing or diving at the instant of release, and at what angle?

Then there were the factors beyond your control: wind speed, cloud cover, the rules of engagement, and — never to be ignored — the enemy's air defense system. To call the best possible air-to-ground play, you had to read the defense. Sometimes you'd come in at medium altitude and roll off into a dive-bomb pattern. In other scenarios you'd do better to scrape the rooftops, jinking and jiving low to the ground. After delivery you'd push into either a steep climb or an aggressive banking turn — both to evade enemy fire and to avoid getting clobbered by your own bomb.

If you missed your target in a dogfight, your seconds on earth might be numbered. But the stakes in hauling iron were no less severe. If you made a bad pass, a squadron mate might have to put *his* life on the line to get the job done. Accuracy was all.

The more training I got in air-to-ground, the happier I was to be slotted for a dual-role airplane. Both missions were demanding, both hugely satisfying. By the time I left Holloman, I'd have been hard-pressed to choose which one I liked most.

And the best was yet to come. In May 1991 I headed out to Luke Air Force Base in Phoenix for the final phase of my schooling. I was about to climb into the most versatile and brilliant multirole fighter ever made.

When the first F-16 was delivered by General Dynamics back in 1978, it marked a revolution in jet design. At the time of its debut, the conventional wisdom was that bigger jets were better and that sophisticated, cutting-edge systems rarely worked. But the F-16 quickly proved that a compact plane with world-of-tomorrow avionics could soar to the head of its class.

More than a decade later, after numerous updates, the F-16 was still going strong. In addition to comprising more than half of the Air Force fighter armada, it ranked as a front-line fighter for more than a dozen of our allies. In training, the F-16 was the safest single-engine fighter in Air Force history. In combat, it was the undisputed champ; through the 1980s, matched up against MiGs and other Soviet-built aircraft in Pakistan and Lebanon, its record was an unblemished 61–0. No other fighter was quite so agile — or quite so user-friendly for the man in the cockpit.

The F-16 could perform like the ultimate sports car yet ride as smoothly as a Fleetwood — and I couldn't wait to get behind the wheel.

From the first time a Luke instructor took me up in a two-seat F-16 trainer version, the T-38 seemed Cro-Magnon by comparison. Where the T-38 had no radar at all, the F-16 stocked a multiuse radar that could detect other planes, map the ground for navigation, and aid in delivering weapons.

Instead of a simple gyro platform, which gives you an artificial horizon but not much more, the F-16's inertial navigation system can pinpoint your position on the earth's surface. Once you feed in the latitude and longitude of your destination, it can instantly tell you what heading to take and how far you have to go.

Where you steer the T-38 with a conventional stick, flight controls in the F-16 are run strictly "fly-by-wire." There are no cables or pulleys; your joystick has no mechanical linkage to any control surfaces. Instead, it sends out an electronic signal to hydraulic actuators, which in turn move the surfaces. (In the earliest F-16s, in fact, the stick didn't move at all; it responded to pressure on different surfaces from the pilot's hand, like the touch-sensitive screen in an automated teller machine. After pilots complained that they missed a sense of "feel," some artificial movement was built in. Even so, steering the F-16 required high finesse and a delicate touch.)

When you manipulate that joystick, you are actually putting in a vote. It is up to the flight control computer to weigh a variety of air data inputs and then decide, within microseconds, whether your vote makes sense. If the plane is hauling too much payload that day to make its sharpest turn, for example, the computer will limit the move before you swing out of control.

In contrast to the T–38's strictly analog, sensor-based instrument panel, the F–16's computer supplies digital readouts for a number of functions. A second computer controlled our weapons systems and cued the pilot to release his missiles or bombs. The computer didn't stop at processing the plane's flight path, altitude, airspeed, and acceleration. It went on to crunch the same data — delivered through radar — for the adversary. I now saw, more than ever, that aerial combat lived within a dynamic, breathing envelope.

At Luke we began to simulate air-to-air combat by "lying" to the computer about weapons that weren't actually loaded on our planes. Our head-up display would tell us when we were within range to "fire" at our make-pretend bandit; a postflight review of the on-board videotape would reveal whether we'd "hit" him.

The F–16 was no less precise as an air-to-ground platform. In one particular system, a targeting pod would zap a laser spot on the ground: X marking the spot. The laser then guided a bomb to its target through a sensor unit that altered the deflection angle of the bomb's fins en route. The accuracy of these bombs was astonishing.

All of these ultrasmart systems made flying the F–16 easier. They were only as effective, however, as the pilot's training and professionalism allowed.

Think of it this way: Suppose they developed a breakthrough tennis racket that could drive a ball 50 percent harder and faster than any on the market today. A racket like that could be exploited to definite advantage — but only by players with strong technique. If you hadn't mastered the skills for the serve and volley, or the cross-court backhand, you'd just be hitting farther out of bounds, maybe conking a guy two courts down.

In the F-16 the pilot still flies the plane. He has computers to guide him, a wealth of indicators to refer to, but it is up to him to set a course and an altitude, to fire a missile or release a bomb. It is his good judgment — and, in a crisis, his ability to improvise — that makes the whole thing work.

The learning curve was steep at Luke. After five rides with an instructor, I soloed. Two rides after that, less than two months into the half-year program, I underwent a watershed test: an instrument checkout, where I demonstrated that I could fly the plane in bad weather.

At the end of that checkout I was officially qualified to fly an F-16. One month later, I joined my class of twenty-one in an initiation ceremony. Students and instructors gathered at the squadron snack bar, where we'd play a pocket billiard game called Crud. There we received our certificates and F-16 patches. And there each of us ate a raw egg, shell and all, and chased it with a shot of Jeremiah Weed, the traditional fighter pilot whiskey.

The egg was crunchy and the whiskey smooth, and I was never more ecstatic.

One Saturday that fall, I went out to a glider field with three of my fellow F-16 students: Brick Izzi, Charlie Moore, and Steve Speckhard. Brick and Charlie were gliding instructors, and they went up together. I took Steve, an old friend from Embry-Riddle, along with me in a second glider; he'd never tried it before.

After this ride, he never would again.

Hoisted by a tow plane to several thousand feet, we went hunting for thermal updrafts, or "good air." They were usually easy to find over the hot Arizona desert, but we petered down to the ground after twenty minutes or so. We got hauled up again, and this time our luck improved — we stayed up for a solid hour. As the rated glider pilot of our team, in the front of the two-seater, I was loving every minute of it. When you're gliding in a clear sky, with strong air, you've no reason to envy the birds.

Just as we prepared to land, we encountered a downdraft — "bad air" — and lots of it. I felt the negative G-force push me up in my seat; we were plummeting toward mother earth at a disturbing rate.

I tried to point the glider's nose down and accelerate out of the downdraft, but this particular patch was bigger than usual. We were under a thousand feet now, and the ground was coming up way too fast.

We were more than a half mile away from the glider field. Worse yet, I saw no place to land: just rocks and brush, and — dead ahead — a busy highway with a string of power lines.

At 500 feet I knew we had less than thirty seconds left aloft. At our present rate and angle of descent, we seemed sure to hit the wires. I didn't lose my cool often, but this was one of those times. "We're not going to make it!" I screamed. At that point Steve didn't feel too good — he'd just come along for the ride, after all.

"You got it, no problem," he lied, and I calmed down. With Steve acting as lookout, we found a gravel road branching off the highway. We finally emerged from the downdraft and cleared the power lines by a hundred feet. I hung a left turn to approach the gravel road, milking the air as best I could.

"Heads up for that tree on the right!" Steve shouted. I lifted the glider's right wing, banking up at a forty-five-degree angle, to avoid a nasty crash. The rest was easy. The landing was on the rough side, but good enough. The plane didn't seem to be damaged. The two of us sat there for a long moment, not saying a word.

"Hey, that's a really good job," Steve piped up from behind me. "Can we get out now?"

By the time we started pushing the glider back to its field, we were laughing hysterically. But those nine lives of mine were dwindling fast.

A few days after New Year's 1992, I landed in Seoul, South Korea, in the dead of night. I'd just been to Martinique with my brother, Paul, my first trip out of the States, but Korea was something else again. As my taxi dodged its way through neon-splashed streets, I felt like I'd fallen into a scene from *Blade Runner*.

After catching some sleep at the Dragon Hill Hotel, a long bus ride delivered me the next evening to Kunsan Air Base, home of the Juvats. I was met by three pilots from the 80th Fighter Squadron, my first operational assignment. Grabbing my bags, they led me straight to the officers' club. On the way they belted out a rendition of "The A.J. Song," to the tune of "Camp Town Races":

A.J.'s going home in a body bag, doo-da, doo-da;
A.J.'s going home in a body bag, oh-de-doo-da-day.
Fighter pilot's dead;
Never found his head;
A.J.'s going home in a body bag, oh-de-doo-da-day.

There were three tiers in the Juvat social hierarchy: the captains and higher-ranking officers, known as fossils; the lieutenants, called punks; and A.J., short for "any Juvat." A.J. was the squadron rookie, its newest member — namely, me. I'd hold on to my unique status until the next new guy came through, whether an hour from now or six months down the road.

A.J.'s main responsibility was to safeguard Woody Juvat, the squadron mascot. Woody was a three-foot-tall statue of an indigenous man standing over an enemy's body, holding up said enemy's head in his right hand — a bow to the 80th's official nickname, the Headhunters. I'd have to keep Woody in my room and take him along to any parties on the base.

Most of all, I'd have to beware of potential kidnappers, particularly from our sister squadron at Kunsan, the Pantons. If someone managed to steal Woody away, I'd have to buy him back with a ransom, some gag that the thief would cook up.

Most of the fighter pilots were at the officers' club that night, Pantons and Juvats both. A bunch of guys were playing Crud, and the songs flowed hot and heavy — we sang songs long into the night. There was no stiffness or reserve among these officers; they took me into their fraternity without missing a beat. By the time that party was over, I felt like I'd been there for weeks.

Kunsan was a remote assignment, a one-year tour with no families allowed, where we all lived together in dorms on the base. While hard on us socially, that year was also a total immersion into fighter pilot culture. We worked and lived together twenty-four hours a day — we had no place else to go. Every night was a hall party, with shared spaghetti suppers and movies on video. The friends you made as a Juvat would be friends for life.

Some people don't realize that we've yet to sign a treaty ending the Korean conflict. We've had a truce for more than forty years, and no one's fighting at the moment, but the war there has never officially ended.

Like other U.S. military units stationed in the country, it was the Headhunters' job to be ready to defend South Korea against an invasion from the North. We performed that task with absolute seriousness. Our main area of responsibility was a prohibited area inside the demilitarized zone, just south of the political border. Talked onto our targets by people on the ground, we'd simulate bombing runs against attacking enemy troops. In close air support, where two sides were fighting on top of each other and battle lines were fluid, 100 percent air-to-ground accuracy was essential — and you couldn't get it without help from the soldiers at the front.

Within a week of my arrival, the whole base shut down tight for a full-scale war exercise — we pretended we were under attack. I was issued my "chem gear," a mask and protective clothing for operations in chemical warfare. There were sirens going off, and blackouts, and people dashing about in armored personnel carriers. It looked real and it felt real.

You flew a lot in Korea, even in normal weeks, but in exercises you'd have "surges" that got you up three times a day. I watched huge airborne packages assembled, one jet taking off on the heels of the next. They'd make quick turns and return to base, reconfigure their weapons systems, refuel, do their maintenance checks, and go right out again for the next sortie.

With the base gearing up for inspection, they staged exercises for six weeks out of my first three months there — a tremendous growing experience, with never a dull moment. I was eager to plunge in, but my indoctrination came first. Whenever a fighter pilot entered a new theater of operations, he had to get smart on the mission at hand: the intel and ops plans, the weapons systems employed there. He might even encounter a different version of the F-16 itself, with a new set of avionics to master.

A month after my arrival, I successfully completed my final check ride. At last I was an operational, mission-ready fighter pilot, ready to go to war or keep the peace.

Kunsan proved a great place to polish my craft. Airspace restrictions were few; in South Korea, noise abatement took a backseat to national defense. We had an uninhabited island at our disposal for bombing target practice, allowing us to conduct "wet" passes with live ordnance. In our air-to-air training, we simulated the highest possible threat in exercises with other F-16s, Marine F-18s, and F-15s out of Kadena Air Base in Okinawa. If we held our own against these planes, we knew we'd measure up to any aggressor.

The American people pay for the best defense in the world, and the core component of defense — even more vital than hardware or technology — is training. A fighter pilot's skills are highly perishable — if you go a month without flying the F-16, an instructor or supervisor must fly with you the next time out. Only constant training keeps you sharp, makes the basics second nature. The least bit of rust can dull a reaction; pause at the wrong time, and you may pay with your life.

In remote assignments, social functions took on added importance. We seized every opportunity to get together, from New Year's to Easter to Thanksgiving. At least once a month we'd throw a "hail-and-farewell" to welcome newcomers and send friends off to their next tour.

You didn't show up in jeans and T-shirts at a hail-and-farewell. Every officer in the squadron — from intel and ops and maintenance as well as the pilots — owned a special party jumpsuit, fashioned by a local tailor. While similar to our flightsuits, they were much more flamboyant: black with gold trim, and decorated with the American flag and squadron patch, plus the wearer's home state flag and sewn-in nickname. As soon as we slipped into those party suits, we kicked back, ready to enjoy ourselves.

Each party had a set order of business, beginning with a cocktail hour. Then we'd move into the mess hall, where we'd introduce any guests and make our toasts: to the commander in chief, the secretary of defense, the chairman of the Joint Chiefs of Staff, the general of the Air Force. Our final toast was with water, to honor fallen comrades, and for a minute our uproarious mood would turn solemn and subdued.

As dinner was served, the rules of the mess took force. Seated at the head — or "cranium" — table was Juvat Lead, our squadron commander, and now both judge and jury. Our criminal code was voluminous and subject to heavy interpretation. Among the common violations: addressing the mess without asking Juvat Lead's permission; sneaking off to the bathroom without same; failing the "nickel check," where all present had to produce the squadron coin; and wearing "unmanly" footwear (cowboy boots and Nikes were in, fuzzy bunny-rabbit slippers out).

After a charge was brought, the accused could attempt some defense — but unless it was wickedly clever, Juvat Lead would throw it out of court. Once convicted, the offender was punished swiftly and without mercy. First he'd march to the back of the mess and dip a glass into the communal grog bowl with his right hand. Then he'd turn around, salute Juvat Lead with his *left* hand, and pay his respects: "To the mess!"

The hard part was drinking it down. The grog bowl might contain *anything*, from apple juice to Tabasco sauce; you'd often see suspicious-looking chunks afloat at the top. At the end you'd turn the glass upside down over your head — it was either drink the concoction or wear it, no exceptions.

As the evening wore on, the mess became more and more litigious. Accusers would begin to embellish their stories or fabricate them entirely. To escalate the hilarity, violators would drag others to the bowl with them. Just as in the sky, a wingman couldn't go to the grog bowl without a flight lead; larger "packages" enlisted a mission commander. If one colonel went up, all the colonels went with him; if a woman was convicted, all the women were roped in. There were times when you'd have half the mess drinking out of the bowl while the other half sat there and laughed at them.

At some point in the evening, someone inevitably jumped up with the Juvat salute, "the snakes": two fists held high and facing one another, like opposing snake heads. "Juvats, what is good?" he'd roar, in a line stolen from *Conan the Barbarian*.

"To crush your enemies," we'd chant back, "to see them driven before you, to hear the lamentations of their women." Now, *that* was one serious icebreaker.

At dinner's end came the speeches. In a mostly futile effort to keep windbags in check, we enforced one more rule: you had to stick your hand in an ice bucket for as long as you spoke. The party would conclude with a big sing-along, led by our squadron choir, of "Twin-Tailed Lightning" and other traditional fighter pilot anthems.

This might sound silly in the retelling, but those parties meant a lot to our esprit de corps in Korea. Without strong personal bonds, the profession of arms becomes fragile at its heart. In a combat environment you needed to trust people, to predict their reactions and rely on their snap judgments. But before you trust people you have to know them. You have to live and work — and laugh — together. As Juvats we did all of that and more; it was the best time of my life.

In March 1993 I was reassigned to the "Black Knights," the 526th Fighter Squadron at Ramstein Air Base in Germany, southwest of Frankfurt. I found an impressive group of pilots and made good friends there, but the social life wasn't quite the same. There were no party suits, no grog bowls — most of the guys had families there to go home to.

As before, I began with an indoctrination for my new theater. At Kunsan our main contingency had been an invasion by North Korea. At Ramstein, though the Iron Curtain had fallen, we prepared for an assault upon Western Europe by Eastern Europe and Russia.

In the process of becoming mission-ready at my new base, I earned my latest Air Force nickname. I was being quizzed by my squadron commander when I consulted the twenty-four-hour bezel on my watch to help solve a time problem. Normally the bezel was set to Greenwich mean time, which we referred to as Zulu time. By some mistake, however, I'd moved it to local Ramstein time, two hours ahead.

When I gave my solution, they told me I was wrong. I was *sure* I'd done everything right — they were trying to trick me, I thought. I held firm; I turned down four or five chances to correct my answer. Finally they showed me what I'd done, from that day forward, my nickname was Zulu.

The year went by in a blur, with a few milestones to remember. I got promoted to captain, which was fairly routine; I reached the five-hundred-hour mark in the F-16.

That summer I rotated down to Turkey, to help enforce a no-fly zone in northern Iraq after Desert Storm. I flew twenty missions for Operation Provide Comfort, which protected Kurdish refugees from Iraqi attacks. While some of my fellow pilots were shot at by SAMs and antiaircraft artillery, I never saw anything come my way.

In May 1994 my standard two-year tour at Ramstein was cut short by Air Force downsizing; the Black Knights were inactivated. Most of our pilots and all of our planes moved down to Aviano, Italy, and became reconstituted as the 555th Fighter Squadron.

The Triple Nickel had a rich and proud history. With roots dating to World War II, it emerged from Southeast Asia in the 1970s as the leading air-to-air squadron in the Air Force, with thirty-nine MiG kills to its credit. It would be an honor to bring the 555th back to life — and a lot of backbreaking work. After serving in temporary duty at Aviano earlier that year, I knew what we'd be up against. Over the next several months we'd work out of prefab buildings and mail slots. In between Deny Flight sorties over Bosnia, we'd put in twelve-hour days at the base: setting up offices, tearing through paperwork, lugging furniture and file cabinets.

To make our task even harder, we were

spread extremely thin; during our off months from Deny Flight, we'd have pilots on four different continents in various exercises and deployments. In February 1995, after stints in Tunisia and Sardinia, I was sent to the States for two months of training. My last stop, in Texas, was for an administrative course on life support, the shop duty I'd be assuming in Aviano that June. It was there that I met Mike Grost and spent two days at his Life Sciences Equipment Laboratory at Kelly Air Force Base.

As far as I'm concerned, Mike is the world's leading authority on life support equipment. In addition to running an active lab for technical postmortems after plane crashes, he'd assembled museum-type displays on the evolution of flight apparel, parachutes, and ejection seats. But the area he brought us to first was a maze of narrow corridors and small partitioned rooms.

Each room contained the aftermath of a jet crash. In some the pilot had ejected successfully, but the fatal mishaps were the ones that locked our eyes. No punches were pulled here. We saw masses of twisted wreckage, smashed seats, mutilated helmets, bloodied flight suits.

We saw everything but the bodies, and Mike passed around photographs of those. His job was to steel us for the very worst scenarios we might encounter back at our squadrons.

I spent half a day sifting through the remains of an F-16 crash from the 1970s. The plane had fallen into a lake during training. The pilot never ejected.

I learned a lot from Mike in those two days: the threshold forces that human bodies could withstand; how our life support systems worked, and the importance of trusting them; and, at the same time, how no piece of equipment was fail-safe. Manual backups had been built in at every step, for the simple reason that things could go wrong.

There was one piece of evidence I'd never forget: the canopy of an F-4 that had bashed another plane in midair. Along the canopy's inner surface, front and rear and all around, I found a number of odd green streaks.

They'd been left there by the pilot's camouflage helmet, Mike explained, as he flailed about the cockpit after the collision. He, too, had failed to eject.

I got the message: When catastrophe struck your plane, get out while the getting was good. If you waited, it was clear, things would only get worse.

CHAPTER FIVE

As my parachute descended to 1,000 feet, the highway lay dead ahead, the idled truck and car a mile or two up the road. With my long ride nearly over, those last few minutes were an agony of waiting.

I made one last effort to steer the chute by heaving on a front riser, but it was no use. I made myself stop staring at the watchers gathered below, and turned to the business at hand: my landing.

A safe parachute landing demands technique, mental discipline, and more than a little good fortune. It's equivalent to a leap from a six-foot platform, and it's easy to get hurt if you don't do it right. At jump school you're taught to keep your head up and legs together, then collapse into a sideways roll along five points of contact: balls of your feet, calf, thigh, hip, and the push-up muscle in your back. When you do it right, your body acts like the rocker of a rocking chair, dispersing the energy of impact.

Mistakes can be costly. Land with your legs apart, and one of them may snap; pull up your feet at the end, and your pelvis or spine could suffer. The injury rate is actually lower for night landings; in daylight, less experienced jumpers will retract their legs by reflex just before touching down.

I'd pared my own technique to the simplest essentials: eyes on the horizon, feet and knees together, knees slightly bent. As long as I stayed relaxed, took the fall as it came, and kept my hands tight on my risers, the rest would follow naturally. In my ten previous jumps, I hadn't so much as pulled a muscle. I didn't intend to spoil my record now, not when a twisted ankle could complicate my evasion.

I could only pray that I'd have a fair shot. I'd done all I could do by twisting my body sideways within the chute, to avoid landing backward and rolling back on my head. The rest was now out of my hands.

As I kept getting blown southeast, my first hurdle was to clear the highway and the cultivated land to its north and west. I made it with a stone's throw of altitude to spare.

At the end the wind did indeed take mercy — or maybe someone greater had a hand at my back. After dangling past two miles' worth of terrain over the course of my drop, I landed just fifty yards beyond the road. Better yet, I wasn't stuck in a tree or exposed in some farmer's backyard. I'd skimmed into a small, empty clearing of foot-high grass, perhaps fifteen feet across and ninety feet deep, with woods all around.

It wasn't paradise, but it would do.

My landing was textbook, if heavy; I fell on my left side like the proverbial sack of potatoes. There was no chute drag, and I stopped clean. The ground was damp and hard. I knew I was in a footrace — I had to make cover before my watchers reached the clearing. Having charted my course from the air; I'd be moving south and away — from the road, from the people — toward the woods.

I quick-released the clips that joined the risers to my harness straps, did the same to the ones that linked my hips to the seat kit. Then my heart hit my sternum. Still inside its plastic bags, my radio had slipped from my vest pocket; the lanyard tethering the bags to me had snaked into the chute lines. It took two seconds to unsnarl it, but I didn't have seconds to spare. The hunters from the highway were coming closer with each breath.

I got a little flustered right there.

Maybe that's why I made my mistake — or maybe I just had too much to deal with in a flash of time. The fact remains that I left behind my hit-and-run auxiliary survival kit within its canvas shell, with my backup radio and half my ration of water inside. I simply forgot it in my haste to get away.

I also left behind my limp parachute — an airman's best friend in more leisurely cases, the canopy good for bedroll or clothing. I ignored the rubber life raft. I swooped down on my survival rucksack, punched a plunger button to free it, and wedged its twenty pounds under my arm like a football. And I ran.

I bolted along the grass and out of the clearing. My path rounded a bend, into a maze of offshoots and turn-backs, around clumps of low bushes and short, skinny trees. I'd thought I could run a marathon, that my flight-or-fight juice would carry me forever, but after thirty seconds I was sucking air. My legs were lead pipes; this whole impossible afternoon had suddenly caved in on me, and my body broke down. I knew I'd be making my trackers' job that much easier, but I had to stop.

I bailed off to the right, into a stand of those aspenlike trees about ten feet square. I dove into the heart of it. The vegetation wasn't as dense as I'd hoped for, with no undergrowth to speak of, but I wasn't feeling choosy. I lay on my left side, in a semifetal position, and propped myself behind a small tree root. The dirt was dark, almost black. Drenched with the sweat of fear and exertion, I could hear vehicles near the point where I'd ditched my parachute — one, two, three of them. The last one rumbled to a stop with the unmistakable, grinding groan of a truck.

The people would be here soon, but I had to take one more stab at reaching my flight lead. If I was going to be captured — and the odds of that seemed pretty fair just now — it was crucial for the Air Force to know I was alive. Having ripped the ziplock bags off my radio, I brought it up to my mouth and pushed a side button to transmit over Guard. Then I stage-whispered as clearly as I could:

"Hey, Wilbur, this is Zulu."

No sooner was my nickname out of my mouth than I heard voices by my parachute. They'd wasted no time.

Again, with my fear-cracked voice: "Hey, Wilbur, this is Zulu." No response. I shut the radio off.

The grass rustled with footsteps, coming my way. Coming with the careless noise of men who know their prey is cornered.

I burrowed my face into the dirt, but the tree root made poor cover. With no time to apply any camouflage paint, I pasted my green synthetic flight gloves over my face and ears, and I froze, barely breathing, willing myself into invisibility.

Not five minutes later came the first ones, striding down the grassy path, speaking some Slavic tongue. I snuck a peek: two men, one white-haired and my height, the other young, maybe eighteen — a grandson? — and slightly taller. They wore rough country clothes and appeared unarmed. They were five yards off and closing.

My face pitched back into the dirt. My heart was thumping in my ears. They came louder with each step. I thought they were sure to see me — how could they miss? — and I knew they had heavy reinforcements. My brain skittered off to what I'd do when I was caught — the best time to escape, I knew, was right after you'd been captured — and then to what *they* might do to me. The armies down here played by their own rules — I had a shattered airplane as proof of that. If I was lucky, I'd get off with a beating, till someone in authority reached the scene and claimed his pawn for the next round of negotiations. And if I wasn't . . .

I remembered a story I'd heard from my survival instructor four years before. During a nighttime evasion exercise, he said, he was sitting on the ground when one of the "enemy" came up and bumped into him. But my instructor stayed still as a post, never murmured a sound — and the other guy walked off, figuring he'd bounced off a tree stump.

"Just don't move," my instructor told me. "Don't assume they see you just because you see them."

I held my breath; I imagined myself blending into the dirt. I wouldn't do their work for them. If they wanted me, they'd have to grab me. They'd have to physically peel me from the ground.

The two men walked to the very edge of my hiding spot, five feet from my burrowed head, and kept going straight down the path, without a hitch in stride or conversation.

I don't know why they missed me — can't explain it, except that God veiled me from them.

I would win many small victories in days to come, but none more gratefully received than that one.

My relief was short-lived, however. Minutes after the first two men passed me by, I heard new stirrings in the vicinity, male voices to both east and west: I was surrounded. Keeping my head down, I looked out as best I could. From my worm's-eye view through the low-hanging branches, I caught intermittent glimpses of backs and legs. They were hiking in groups of two and three, poking about the brush, calling out to one another. At times they were no more than ten feet away from me. Over the next hour I'd count about fifteen of them, but I heard what might have been dozens more rushing past on either side.

Like the first pair, these men wore civilian clothes, but they'd brought along something extra: each one of them hefted a rifle. That sight was a knife to my spine. I had yet to spot a single squirrel or rabbit in these woods. I knew this party had bigger game in mind.

I stopped worrying about getting beaten up, about becoming a hostage, about torture or solitary confinement.

These men were out to kill me.

It was cold comfort that they weren't in uniform; rogue paramilitaries might be that much less restrained.

There was nothing to do but to pray. I prayed to my O'Grady grandparents and to my Aunt Ellen, my godmother, claimed far too young by cancer — if they had any clout with the Big Guy upstairs, would they see what they could do? I called on Jesus and Mary, on every saint and apostle I could think of. *I'm not ready to die, but if I must, please forgive my sins and let me go to heaven.*

I tried to say the rosary but lost track of

the sequence without my rosary beads. I remembered another prayer, an old favorite. For me it captured God's infinite capacity for love and forgiveness: *Dear Lord, I am not worthy, but only say the word and I shall be healed* . . .

That's when I heard the first rifle shot, much too close, echoing through the woods. That's when I got more frightened than I'd ever been in my life. I scarcely flinched — I'd hold my dirt-eating post here as long as they'd let me — but I genuinely believed I was about to die. The Lord's Prayer came into my mind.

Our Father, who art in heaven, hallowed be Thy name . . .

They say young people think they're bulletproof, but I knew better — I'd seen too much death in the sky. In my brief time with the Air Force, I'd known four pilots lost to bad luck or bad weather or some malfunction that defied the best maintenance in the world. None of them died in combat; it didn't take a war to make our business risky. But until you faced it foursquare, death remained a tragedy that happened to someone else.

Trust me, I was facing it now.

Thy kingdom come, Thy will be done, on earth as it is in heaven . . .

Another shot and a pinging ricochet — this

one might have struck a rock. It ran through me like high voltage. Were they trying to flush me out? Or just shooting at the slightest quiver of a branch or bush, hoping to find me behind it? I worried about the torn ziplocks. They were under my leg, but I couldn't quite cover them completely, and there was still light enough to bounce off the plastic and into a prying eye.

Give us this day our daily bread, and forgive us our trespasses, as we forgive those who trespass against us . . .

When people talked about life passing before their eyes, I'd always thought it would look like a home movie. But for me it was a slide show, a series of stills. The first person I pictured was an old girlfriend. Boy, I thought, had I messed up. She was the only girl I'd ever loved, and I think she once loved me, but my head was literally in the clouds in those days. All I could think about was becoming a fighter pilot, and I wanted no baggage along my merry way.

When I saw her years later, I fell in love all over again, but it was too late; our lives had unraveled too far to be knit back together. But it made me question whether the path I'd picked — the one I'd always been so sure of — had truly been best for me. Would I be happier if I'd grabbed that girl and become a postal worker in Pocatello, Idaho? I'd lived a full life in twenty-nine years; I'd traveled to five continents, seen and done things most people can't imagine. But I wasn't ready to die — I wasn't *finished* yet. I so much wanted to be a husband and a father, and now it looked like I'd never have the chance . . .

And lead us not into temptation, but deliver us from evil . . .

Then again, I was truly thankful not to be married — not on this day, on this patch of killing ground. I was glad that the missile hadn't gotten one of the married pilots, leaving a wife back in Italy in torment. In January a pilot from the 510th, Mark "Mac" McCarthy, one of the top men in the entire wing, had flown his final, fatal sortie — just a routine, daytime air-to-air exercise. The whole base had been down in the dumps ever since. But the worst part of it was that Mac had a wife and two little ones, two very young children who wouldn't have their dad.

Another shot, another crackle inside me. Were they getting closer? *Just don't move.*

I thought about my own dad back in Alexandria, Virginia, and prayed that I wouldn't die before he did — that I would get to be with him again. I'd give up all my worldly wealth for that; I'd start all over, take my old job as a dishwasher. I flashed to the blue suiters, the chaplain and the rest, knocking on his front door to deliver the dread news; I could feel my dad's hurt. I pictured the same scene played out with my mother in Seattle.

I envisioned the next funeral we'd all be attending, down to the eulogy and pallbearers, and it was eerie to know it would be my own.

A great sadness welled over me, and soundlessly I cried. I felt a single tear track down my cheek and into the dirt.

It was the first and last tear I'd allow myself in Bosnia.

My mom, Mary Lou Scardapane, had just mailed off a last note to me, to ask if there was anything I needed. She'd be coming to Italy the next week with her husband, Joseph, and her ninety-seven-year-old father-in-law, Felix Scardapane, who had relatives in the country. On the morning of June 2, as she joined Felix to work in their backyard garden, he asked her, "Have you spoken with your son this morning?"

She assumed it was some question about their trip, until Felix added, "A plane is down — an F-16."

My mom was furious but not fearful. It couldn't be me — they'd be seeing me in Aviano, the reservations were all set. But just to check, she called her brother Michael, a staff sergeant at McChord Air Force Base, to see what he knew about it. She left a message on his machine and had no sooner cradled her phone than it rang.

It was my dad. Though my parents had divorced several years before, they'd remained friends. But my mom knew instantly that this call wasn't routine — my father was so broken, so distraught. He managed to get out, "Mare, the Air Force has been here —"

"He's not dead, he's not dead, he's not dead!" my mother screamed, and then she looked out her window and saw the three men in blue suits mounting the path to her front door. Just as they did in the war movies, when they delivered the very worst news, when they solemnly reported that the young man who belonged to you wasn't coming home . . .

She told my father she'd call him back and opened the door. A trim young man — an Air Force major, it turned out — began trying to explain something, but my mother wouldn't let him. She cut him off with the words that she'd hang her whole being on for days to come.

"He's not dead, he's not dead, he's not dead —"

The phone rang: my uncle calling back. "Mike," my mom said, "they're here. What do I do?"

"It's okay, sis. They're there to help you. Just let them."

What was it that I'd once told her, to soothe her qualms about my flying a fighter jet? *This is my job — this is what I do.* She'd been proud of me, of course, but she'd always had that nagging whisper, that small misgiving, wrapped up in some corner of her subconscious. Now the whisper had burst from its box and grown into a brain-splitting roar, like some science fiction monster run amok. And the worst of it was that the roar was inside her, and she knew she had no place to hide.

My mom went back to her door and invited the three men in: a chaplain, a doctor, and the major, who handed her a letter from the Air Force Military Personnel Center.

On behalf of the Chief of Staff, United States Air Force, it is with deep personal concern that I officially inform you that the status of the whereabouts of your son, Captain Scott F. O'Grady, has been unknown since approximately 10:00 A.M. this morning. Scott was participating in a routine flight in support of Operation Deny Flight in or around the former land area of Yugoslavia. He was the pilot of the F-16C aircraft that was apparently shot down by a surface to air missile.

There was no visible sign of a parachute and no contact has been made with Scott since the incident. . . .

My mother glanced at the letter, but she wouldn't read it through. She wouldn't read it, and at first she thought she'd tell no one about it. Not even her two other children, because once you told someone else, it was real, and it *couldn't* be real — she wouldn't let it be real . . .

I heard half a dozen close rifle shots through that first afternoon and men passing about me for the better part of two hours. The miracle is that not one of them spotted me. After a time the voices grew fainter. I dared not stir; I could still hear people out toward the parachute, and many more had trod past me into the woods than had come back out.

By six o'clock I felt bold enough to try my radio: "Anyone, Basher Five-Two." With static as my answer, I knew I wouldn't be rescued that day and felt a twinge of disappointment. Just three hours ago, I'd been flying in a perfectly sound aircraft. Not so long before that, I'd been sipping a cappuccino on the patio of my village café. My mother was set to visit me in just a few days; my father was supposed to be coming in October. The last two weeks of July were blocked off for Spain, where I was to join my sister and brother on our annual siblings' escapade. Our family was far-flung now — Stacy taught junior high in Chicago, Paul was about to enter dental school in North Carolina — but we were close.

Now all those plans meant nothing. Now that plane was so much landfill, and its pilot someone's target practice, too scared to show a sliver of his face.

Now I might never see my family again.

I wished for a time machine back to the day before, to take Brick Izzi up on his offer of ground alert — it looked like I might not get to spend the $150 bonus, anyway. I wished I could make my way to the highway and flag down a sympathetic motorist. "You look like you need some help," he'd say. "Why don't you come home with us — we'll get you a good meal, and you can call your friends. You'll spend the night, and tomorrow they'll come and pick you up . . ."

Snap out of it, jerko! I'd had a spasm of denial, just a tiny tic, but I couldn't give in to it. I had much to do and far to go before I could feel safe, and I'd never make it if I lost touch with the facts of my new life:

I was here.

This was real.

My next mistake might be my last.

At seven o'clock my bowels gave way, flooded my pants — my stress had found a release. For the time being I'd have to live with it; the days in June lasted forever in this part of the world, and I wouldn't risk any big motions until dark. I wondered about my nagging burns. Gingerly extracting my Swiss Army knife from my flight suit chest pocket, I unhinged the broadest blade and held it to my face for a mirror. My cheeks had blistered, and the fire had singed off my eyelashes and part of my eyebrows. I felt relieved — I'd been worried that half my face had melted off. There was a first-aid kit in another pocket, but I wasn't about to dig for some ointment; it was packed inside one of those noisy plastic bags, and I had a vow of silence to keep.

I lightly fingered the little silver cross around my neck. Stacy had given it to me after I'd graduated from pilot training and been assigned to the F-16. The design was unusual, with a dove at the cross's center. "Here's something to protect you," she'd said. I'm not superstitious — I don't believe in charms or talismans — but I treasured that cross as a symbol of my faith, of who I was and what I believed in. Stacy and I have our political disagreements — she's the most liberal person in our family, and I'm probably

132

the most conservative — but both of us are striving for a peaceful world.

In fact, there's no group that craves peace more than our people in uniform; we're the ones whose lives are on the line, after all. I happen to believe that we need a strong military to keep that peace and to shield it from aggressors. That philosophy led me into the Air Force — and, I thought ruefully, got me where I was today.

Letting the cross drop, I had a queasy feeling. I ran a mental check for my Saint Christopher's medallion in my flight suit pocket. I'd gotten it years ago from Maggie O'Brien, the mother of a high school friend in Spokane. Christopher was the patron saint of travelers, and I wouldn't make a Deny Flight sortie — or even a commercial flight — without it.

I felt my right chest pocket — wasn't there. Tried my left — ditto. The medallion was missing. I'd somehow left it back in my locker, with my wallet.

I pressed on with my inventory, to see what else was missing. There was my flight jacket, of course, now a big regret. It had been cool when I landed, and now it was getting downright chilly.

Then I saw my plastic Geneva Convention ID card — sitting in Aviano, in my truck's overhead visor. All I had on me for identification were my dog tags and my captain's stripes, sewn into the shoulders of my flight suit. The ID card affirmed my rights to humane treatment under the Convention; I hoped I wouldn't need it.

And there was one item that I normally didn't wear over Bosnia, that I wished I hadn't brought today — my Rolex watch, a keepsake from my father. Whatever else might happen if I was captured, that watch would be gone in a heartbeat.

But I refused to kick myself for any of these things. It would do no good to get demoralized. If there was one quality that separated successful evaders from those who cracked, it was self-confidence — the conviction that you could overcome any obstacles and do what needed to be done.

I knew, too, that the Lord indeed worked in mysterious ways. Had I waited for my parachute to deploy automatically, for example, the wind would have had less time to blow me southeast. I could well have landed to the north side of the road, easy pickings for the nearest shooter, and the second guesses would all have been moot.

I stayed stock-still behind my tree root well into darkness, long after I'd heard the last searcher leave my landing area. Noise carries farther in the dark; a dry twig can crack like a cherry bomb. I watched a few lights in the distance to the north. After you stare at a light long enough, even a still one will seem to move, and I was left to guessing.

Were they house lights? Searchlights? Flashlights, with dogs trotting alongside?

Were they coming back to look for me?

After six hours in the same position, I could chart every pressure point in my body: elbows, hips, knees. But stiffness and discomfort weren't much to bear, not when you weighed them against a bullet in your forehead. I'd never bagged a deer, but I'd done enough hunting to know that people watched for the motion, not the animal. *Just don't move.*

I thought of my squadron mates in Aviano, home safe with their families, just two hundred miles away as the crow flies — and a galaxy removed from what I was facing.

Finally, toward midnight, I resolved to move on. There were risks in going, but it seemed out of the question to wake up in a hide site so close to the highway. I would go south, toward higher, more remote ground, as I'd planned while in my chute.

But first I had some housekeeping. I wouldn't be needing the torn ziplocks (useless and noisy), my harness with its metallic clips (too visible), or my sodden underwear. Everything else I'd lug with me, including the full rucksack; this was not the time or place to sort out survival gear.

I carefully unstrapped my harness, then unzipped the top of my G-suit down my right side, pausing at each metal tooth. It was how I'd proceed throughout my time in Bosnia, taking everything as slowly and quietly as I could, spending minutes on functions that normally took seconds or less.

I folded the G-suit back, to get at my flight suit and the zipper at my crotch. Next I partly unzipped my survival vest, to retrieve my Swiss Army knife from out of my flight suit. (I also had a standard-issue, U.S.-made knife, but I knew from experience that it was a piece of junk — it couldn't hold an edge.)

I was about to cut off my underwear — to slice down from the waistband to each leg hole — when I recollected a story about a pilot friend of mine at Ramstein Air Base in Germany. He'd been flying to enforce a no-fly zone over northern Iraq when he got the runs. While flying back to Turkey, where we were temporarily based, he'd tried to cut off his underwear and start cleaning up. He almost passed out when his knife hand came back covered with blood; he thought he'd lost his future generations. It turned out that he'd just nicked a finger — but I took it as a cautionary tale.

I made my cuts and rolled to my back. Grabbing my shorts in the middle, I pulled them through and dropped them to the dirt beside me. I was still a mess inside my flight suit, but my next shower would take some earning. I zipped up my flight suit, zipped back my G-suit, zipped up my survival vest — slowly, slowly, as before.

Still lying on my back, I struggled out of my harness and spent the next several minutes trying to shift it over the plastic bags and underwear, with the harness clips concealed. I wanted to make my trash pile tough to discover, to keep them busy digging for a while. But that got to be too tricky and too noisy, and I gave it up. I'd let them find this much, and no more — I'd leave no further trace in any other location, to prevent them from connecting the dots. Littering could be hazardous to my health.

Now I faced my toughest task yet: getting up off the ground. Anyone blessed with a healthy body does this every day, without thinking, but it's a whole different enterprise when you must do it without a sound.

I started by rolling back to my left side, then pushing my torso up slow-motion with my right hand. With my left hand anchored, I pivoted into a sitting position. Then I brought my legs in close; both hands were flat on the dirt behind me now, to help lift me into a squat.

Each of these moves had half a dozen components, and I isolated each one; the muscle strain was tremendous. In between them I'd stop, listen, and look around. I'd freeze like a mannequin for a minute or more — longer if I'd scraped a branch or leaf, longer still if I'd stepped on a dead branch, which would go off like a land mine.

I was glad I'd been hitting the stair-step machine for the past few weeks — I could see I'd be needing the stamina.

I grabbed my survival rucksack, nice and slow, rose up to a hunch, and took five baby steps out of the trees and onto the grass. It took me a solid hour to get out of that hide site. When I finally stood upright, it was a strange, trembling sensation. My body had forgotten what it felt like to relax.

Just then it crossed my mind that there might be Bosnian Serb troops with night-vision goggles out there — that any outfit with the skill and technology to total an F-16 could have a few more tricks in store for me. But I had no choice. I stepped out on the grass and off into the unknown.

The night was dead silent and dark as a tomb; I could count the stars on one hand. I stuck to my protocol, taking one step at a time, often swaying on the uneven terrain: stop, look, listen. It was like that kids' game, red-light, green-light, where you freeze in your tracks when the caller whirls around.

Back inside the winding maze, I skirted the edge of other deciduous tree clumps or thicket patches, relying on my internal compass to steer away from the road. All I could see were shades of gray: lighter gray for paths, darker gray for foliage. All I could hear was my own rough breathing. When I paused, I'd hold my inhale, just to make sure I wasn't missing something.

After ten minutes my path widened, and the trees around it grew taller, to about twenty-five feet. I found myself on a mild easterly decline, to where I could no longer see the lights around the highway, a reassurance. But then I hit a dead end and had to double back, and took a twist to the south again.

This time the path narrowed and turned slightly uphill, and I found myself at a small cul-de-sac. It was a grassy cove the size of a kitchen, with a few bushes in the middle and those skinny trees all around, extending out for some length. It felt out of the way — a good place to be. I hadn't planned to go far this first night, in any case. I'd wanted only to get the lay of the land, locate a safer refuge, and attempt to make radio contact.

I walked into the small clearing and zipped open my rubberized rucksack. Here is what I found: eight flexipaks of water, a total of one quart; an empty plastic water pouch; a wool ski hood; a pair of woolen socks; a pair of green wool mittens; a floppy orange and green hat; a thin vinyl tarp, green on one side, silver on the other; a four-foot square of black and brown camouflage netting; a bright foil space blanket; a pair of sun goggles and a bottle of sunblock lotion, SP 15; a magnesium bar fire starter; a five-inch knife; and a 121-page, waterproof booklet entitled "Aircrew Survival."

For me it was a mixed bag. I could use the water, tarp, and clothing; the rest of it was probably excess baggage. I knew, in particular, that I was unlikely to snuggle up with "Aircrew Survival." I doubted I'd have any leisure time for reading; my common sense and training would guide me for now.

I checked the pockets of my survival vest. Besides my radio and medical kit, they contained a variety of flares, a compass, a whistle, a camouflage stick, a tourniquet, a wire snare, and the GPS navigational receiver. Holstered in place was my 9-mm Beretta. I decided against chambering a round from the gun clip. Given the numbers I was up against,

I'd be hard-pressed to win any shoot-out.

Sitting on the rucksack, I slipped on the ski mask and exchanged my soaked cotton socks for the woolen pair, which would insulate better even when wet.

Then I took out the GPS; I needed a fix on my position before I could do much good on the radio. Blindfolded by the night, I managed to get it started up, but its batteries were about dead. I took the spare set from the receiver's case — four double-As — and made the switch. In the process, two of the old batteries fell into the grass — a small crisis, since I knew I couldn't leave them there. I reached down and grabbed one out of blind luck, but the other eluded me. Moving very slowly, just as before, I unzipped the shoulder pocket on my flight suit. I removed a penlight and flicked it once toward the ground.

The beam was so bright, so white, that it scared me. I tried muting the light with a red plastic filter, but then I couldn't see the ground. I risked a third half-second flash, and this time I caught the metal's glint.

The size of a Walkman, the GPS could reliably calculate the holder's position to within one hundred feet. The catch was that it relied on triangulation and needed to align with — or "ring up" — three satellites to get a useful read. You might get all three within seconds, but it could also take five minutes or more.

On this night it seemed to take forever to ring up the first one. I cupped my hand over the GPS screen to mask its illumination; every minute or two I stole a quick glance. At last I saw the magic message — "1 SATELLITE" — on the liquid crystal display. After fifteen minutes I had the trio, and my latitude and longitude read out to three decimal places: a major triumph.

I might still be in the middle of no-man's-land, but at least I could tell people how to get there.

I brought out my radio. Wilbur would be home with Sharon by now — sick at heart, to be sure, but out of the picture. To cast a wider net, I used my formal call sign on Guard: "Anyone, Basher Five-Two." I'd rehearsed my brief message in my head. It *had* to be brief; any hostile party with the proper equipment could track me after ten seconds of transmission.

"Anyone, Basher Five-Two."

Once again I got static as reply. I wasn't surprised. Our $4,000 radios can do a lot of things, but they work by line-of-sight contact. A mountain or hill might be blocking my signal.

I'd come through so much just to get to this cove in the woods, yet my ordeal showed no signs of ending. No one knew where I was or even whether I'd survived.

For all that, I felt calm, even content. I wasn't quite the same person who'd taken off from Aviano twelve hours before. I'd been through the crucible that day, through terror and the smell of death, and come through in one piece. There would be scares ahead, no doubt, but somehow I sensed that I'd never be afraid in that same, stark way again — not in Bosnia, not anywhere.

And that I'd never again feel so alone.

I'd had a revelation that afternoon. While I'd found peace with God long before, my belief had never been put to so hard a test. Those rifle shots had tempered my faith, like strokes from a blacksmith's hammer; those trembling hours in the woods had cemented it. I'd learned that I could turn to God at the very worst times and that He would never desert me.

There is a parable about a man who once dreamed that he was walking along a beach with God. When he turned his head to glance behind him, he saw two sets of footprints in the sand: one his, the other God's. But when he gazed back farther, to look over his whole life's journey, he saw there were stretches with only one set of prints — and that these coincided with the saddest times of his life.

The man called up to God with a note of reproach in his voice: "Lord, you pledged that you'd walk with me all the way once I decided to follow you. But now it seems that you left me when I needed you most."

"My precious child," God replied, "I would never leave you. When you suffered most, in those times that you see but a single set of footprints, it was then that I carried you."

Now I understood that I, too, had been carried.

What's more, I was alive to rejoice in it.

I was a survivor.

CHAPTER SIX

Time was on my side as long as it stayed dark, and I used it to scout for the best possible evasion shelter — what the survival trainers call a hole-up site. I remembered the *BLISS* principle: a hole-up should *b*lend into its surroundings; be *l*ow and regular *i*n *s*hape; set in a *s*ecluded area. My wish list also included a decent angle for observation, an avenue for escape, a good spot for radio reception, and protection from the elements.

When you're on the run, however, you become open to compromise — you take what you can get and try to do better the next time. From the clearing I walked thirty feet into the forest, wincing at the noise of my footsteps. I stopped when I found some trees slightly thicker than the rest; they'd offer some concealment if I got in tight against them. I folded over my tarp so that only the green side showed, lay on top of it, and pulled what was left over me. Next came my netting, spread over the tarp. Everything was too small; my feet stuck out at the end. I used my rucksack for a pillow, minding that its zipper and silver vent hole faced down.

Sometime past four o'clock I tried two more radio calls — no go. After I'd finished my chores, and it was starting to get light, I broke out a flexipak of water, my first liquid in seventeen hours. That initial sip tasted better than the freshest orange juice or the smoothest Belgian beer. I made the four ounces last, sucking lightly from the small hole I'd torn in the top of the pack. Should I have one more?

No, I'd wait.

It wasn't till dawn broke that I saw how the night had tricked me. The deeper I'd delved into the forest, the sparser the low branches; I had little cover from anyone entering the cul-de-sac. I made a quick judgment call — I'd get a new hole-up site, and fast. Collecting my gear, I headed back toward the clearing, to a spot where the undergrowth was denser. The same drill, at the same torpid — and now nerve-grinding — pace: tarp, netting, rucksack. I broke a branch off a tree, gently bending it till it gave, and placed it over my bedding for additional camouflage.

When I finished, my head was propped on a slight incline, the better to see out. It was also no more than three feet from the edge of the grass. Sleep was hopeless. My mind spun like a racing engine; it wouldn't shut off. Keeping a hawk's eye on the clearing, I retrieved my evasion chart from my G-suit pocket. I wanted to plot the coordinates I'd gotten from my GPS and find out my location, the first step toward a rescue mission.

The chart, known as an EVC in the trade, was actually a topographical map of Bosnia, printed in camouflage colors, with added features along its margins: first-aid advice, navigation pointers, and pictures and descriptions of edible plants, complete with vitamin content.

The EVC was made out of Tyvek, a heavy-duty, waterproof material that could substitute for tar paper in housing construction. As the margin notes pointed out, the chart had many ingenious uses: as a blanket or cape for shelter, a bag for hauling food, a splint for a broken wrist, even a plug for a sucking chest wound.

But for me the EVC had two drawbacks: it was huge, about five feet by three, and it was about fifty times as loud to handle as your morning newspaper. I couldn't keep unfolding the map before each move, so I cut it along a fold with my Swiss Army knife; I'd use the smaller portion to navigate around my immediate area, and stow away the rest.

When I'd finally plotted my coordinates, I saw that the big hill I'd targeted was two miles south of where I'd landed — a healthy hike, given the likely pitfalls along the way.

You'd be surprised at how busy a lone man can keep in one little spot in the woods — I felt like I was juggling three hot potatoes. I ran a constant mental check on my equipment, with special emphasis on items I'd withdrawn from the rucksack. Every time my foot twitched I needed to check the tarp, to make sure the silver side wasn't showing. To shift from my right side to my back for relief was a major production, in three acts; in this still, cool air, a stirring branch would stick out like a flag.

Then there was the unavoidable act of urination, a big-time challenge. I'd slowly roll to my side, away from the tarp, inch up the zipper of my flight suit, and aim as well as a man can from a prone position.

I had no lack of incentive to be careful in my work. I'd heard the nightmare stories about American POWs in Vietnam and other places. Capture led to any number of things, most of them ugly. I would do anything I could to avoid it.

I was glad of my efforts later that morning when the sound of two male voices — in oh-so-casual conversation — wafted toward me.

They grew more distinct, and then I knew they were headed for my cul-de-sac. I turned my face toward the ground, my nose flat on the tarp, my eyes clamped shut, leaving only my gray ski mask in view. I pressed my feet flush to the ground, curled my legs to my chest. The steps came nearer, the voices ever louder, until the two men were as close as the grass allowed, as close as the old man and the youth had been the day before, a mere five feet from my rooted head —

Hail Mary, full of grace. The Lord is with thee . . .

— and they never stopped. Soon I heard them trail away from me. I'd been expecting some visitors — it stood to reason that the ones who'd found my parachute would be back. It would have been easy enough to round up more people and cart them down the highway toward the spot where I'd landed. By tomorrow their job would be harder. They'd have to extend the range of their search; they'd have to give me credit for moving farther out.

Meanwhile, I was still at large. Still alive.

In the middle of an overcast afternoon, I heard the roar of a helicopter rotor from the west, flying low. Was it one of ours? But that was wishful thinking, promptly disposed of.

NATO couldn't know where to begin to look for me.

The chopper closed ground, skimming the trees. It was a Gazelle, the bad guys' brand. It flew so low that I could see the two men inside. I wasn't overly worried about them, even when they passed overhead. As still and well hidden as I was, I'd have to be very unlucky to be seen from above.

But that helicopter meant that the Bosnian Serbs had raised the ante. I was an important person in these parts. They were tracking me from the air now as well as on the ground. If I'd ever been tempted to move before nightfall, the sight of that Gazelle put the kibosh on it.

The chopper left my vicinity after fifteen minutes, but it rattled inside my brain for some time after. I felt shaken by all this attention, by the forces out there pursuing me.

And then I shut my eyes, and something happened to make me realize that I wasn't outnumbered, after all — that I had more allies than I could count. I prayed, and I wasn't a solo. I had joined a huge chorus; I could hear prayers for me from throughout the world, from my family to the most remote, faceless stranger. There were no barriers of language, or politics, or even religion. There was only a rising tide of unity, and caring, and belief.

With so many behind me, how could I not prevail?

The woods quieted. Toward six o'clock I made out the lowing of cows; they were miles away, but I could hear them clearly. For the wary ear, there was activity all around — the bark of a dog, the rush of a truck's tires, and, as the day wore on, the sporadic spray of gunfire. Bosnia was a beautiful country, but you could never forget it was a war zone.

Barring contact from a friendly source, I'd ruled out talking on the radio by day. But I was able to listen in silence by plugging in my earpiece. Every so often, whenever I found the time, I'd tune in to Guard and Alpha.

I never monitored for more than a few minutes at a stretch. I had to be cautious with my battery life, but it was also a matter of first things first. In a survival situation, your lead priority was just that: to *survive*. Next came concealment and evasion, and only afterward communication and rescue plans.

According to our military code of conduct, which governed behavior by U.S. evaders and prisoners of war, we were never to surrender of our own free will. The motto of my own 31st Fighter Wing echoed the courage of so many POWs, living and dead: "Return with Honor."

That motto was sacred to me. Surrender in Bosnia was not an option. As much as I wanted to be safe, I was ready to hold out and resist — to do all in my bodily power to stay free until I made my way back to friendly forces.

But at the same time, had I been critically wounded — if I were sure to die without medical attention — it was my *duty* to survive. In that kind of crisis, I'd have reached out to the first person I encountered, produced my blood chit, and asked for medical help as an act of mercy. If that led to my capture, I'd then do what I could to escape, as soon as I was able.

But survival came first. If I failed in that, I'd be failing myself and my nation.

So I had to keep evading, to rivet my energy on that difficult job, even if it meant that I couldn't monitor the radio every minute. If I was caught, after all, my friends from Aviano wouldn't hear from me anytime soon.

As the sun fell on my second day on the ground, I came to feel more settled. I had made it this far, learning as I went; I was ready to stay out a lot longer. It was a matter of accepting reality. When your airplane got shot down, you naturally landed on top of the

(*ABOVE*) Me with my two heroes, my dad and my brother, Paul. (*Author photo*)

(*LEFT*) Me and my mom at Nellis Air Force Base in May 1994. (*Photo courtesy of Mary Lou Scardapane*)

Sitting in my F-16. *(Author photo)*

My grandparents, Frank and Dorothy, and me posing in front of my F-16. *(Photo courtesy of Mary Lou Scardapane)*

I went bobsledding with Paul and Stacy in Cortina, Italy, for Christmas in 1994. The truck replaced the BMW I totaled nine months earlier in Italy. (*Author photo*)

The caption reads "To Mom: My office!" *(Photo courtesy of Mary Lou Scardapane)*

The men to whom I owe my life. Members of the 24th Marine Expeditionary Unit (SOC), who participated in the TRAP mission, clean their weapons on their return to the USS *Kearsarge.* *(Photo courtesy of USMC Corporal Kurt Sutton)*

Returning from Bosnia, two CH-53Es from the 24th MEU (SOC) prepare to land on the flight deck of the USS *Kearsarge*. *(Photo courtesy of USMC Sergeant Dave Garten)*

Just off the rescue helicopter, onto the deck of the USS *Kearsarge*. *(Photo courtesy of USMC Sergeant Dave Garten)*

With Lieutenant General Michael E. Ryan, commander of the Allied Air Forces in southern Europe. *(Photo courtesy of AP/Wide World Photos)*

I was overcome with emotion at the press conference. Captain T.O. Hanford's voice was the first I heard when I was trying to make contact. *(Photo courtesy of AP/Wide World Photos)*

With my family upon my return to the United States. *(Photo courtesy of AP/Wide World Photos)*

The Juvats sign. *(Photo courtesy of AP/Wide World Photos)*

With Captain Bob "Wilbur" Wright, who was flying with me when I was shot down. *(Photo courtesy of AP/Wide World Photos)*

With President Clinton and General John Shalikashvili, chairman of the Joint Chiefs of Staff. *(Photo courtesy of AP/Wide World Photos)*

shooters, which made for a strong possibility that anyone coming in for you would be shot down as well. To put a safe package out there — to organize the different players and co-ordinate their mission — took time. It wasn't like *Star Trek;* we didn't have transporters to phase guys back from hostile territory. I trusted the will and talent of our military, never wavered in that, but I also knew that they wouldn't come out here half-cocked.

If all broke right, I might get picked up tomorrow. But I thought a week's wait was more likely, and I decided, then and there, to steel myself to evade for forty-five days. If I wasn't rescued by then, I'd go on for forty-five more. It wouldn't do any good to set a deadline; I'd just be setting myself up for a fall.

There were many people, after all, who'd survived far longer — and far worse. I thought of the South American football team whose plane had crashed in the Andes, into cold that made Bosnia tropical, and how they'd stayed alive for months by eating the flesh of dead teammates. I thought of our hostages in Lebanon, who'd endured years of captivity. I thought of Lance Sijan, the Vietnam-era Air Force pilot who ejected in the mountains of Laos. With no food and little water, Sijan had crawled through the jungle for six weeks on a mangled leg. Even after he was captured by North Vietnamese soldiers, he was somehow able to overpower his guard and escape briefly. Through two more weeks of interrogation and torture, Sijan would divulge not a shred of military information — a silence he kept to his death in Hanoi.

The life and death of Lance Sijan put my current predicament into some perspective.

At bottom, I realized, it wasn't just luck or circumstance that predicted how people fared in survival situations. It was their inner strength, their determination, their power of will.

By strange coincidence, I'd read a magazine article titled "The Will to Survive" just before dressing for my mission the day before — it was tacked up in the men's room of the life support shop. The story cited two extreme cases. The first involved a man who'd been stranded eight days in the Arizona desert without food or drink. He traveled more than 150 miles in the heat of the day. He lost 25 percent of his body weight from lack of water. A 10 percent loss is usually fatal. His blood was so thick that his lacerations could not bleed.

That man had made every mistake in the book. Yet he survived — not because he was a survival expert, but because he refused to die.

The second story was about a civilian pilot who landed on a frozen Canadian lake after his engine failed. Unhurt, he saw a wooded shoreline only two hundred yards distant, a likely source of food and shelter. He started off and made it halfway there. But then he turned back to his cockpit, smoked a cigar, took out his pistol, and put a bullet in his brain. For some reason the pilot had despaired. He'd lost his will to survive.

Less than twenty-four hours later, a rescue team came upon his body.

I knew I'd have to keep moving — that my hole-up site was still too close to my parachute and the road. But I decided to wait one more day, to gather myself and try to place the distant voices, the people I'd need to avoid in transit. That night I called out on the radio another two or three times. I slept fitfully, ten or twenty minutes at a stretch. Combat naps, we call them, when your mind stays on guard and rousts you at the smallest sound.

It was Sunday — a wonderful day back in Italy, a time for soccer games and long lunches. My cupboard, however, was bare. Rations weren't issued in survival kits for this theater, and I'd never bothered to pack my own cereal bars. From a strictly physiological standpoint, I knew that food was over-rated; a healthy person can function for up to thirty days without it. I was confident I'd be able to find sustenance in the wild long before that point.

At the moment, though, the pickings looked slim. I hadn't seen any wild fruit, not so much as a berry. While inside my tarp that morning, I stripped a leaf off a nearby tree for inspection. It was smaller than a stick of gum, oval-shaped and pointed at the end. There is a rigorous, five-step edibility test for strange flora. You start by rubbing the plant on the outside of your lip, then on the inside, and then you hold it in your mouth for five minutes before you even think of swallowing. At the first sign of itching, burning, or nausea, you send it back, move on to the next course.

My own technique wasn't that scientific. I ate one leaf; an hour later, after no ill effects, I sampled two or three more. I plucked them off one at a time, to avoid shaking their branch. I tried to be a smart consumer — I went for the clean leaves, skipped over the ones with those little brown spots.

The leaves didn't have much taste, and the chewing dried my mouth out something awful. I remembered an old lesson — that digestion saps water from your system — and declared breakfast to be over.

In survival training they tell you to "ration sweat, not water" — that the best place to store water is in your stomach. You're supposed to drink what you think you need when you have it, and reduce your demand for fluids by cutting back on physical activity. Once you get dehydrated, you don't think as clearly. You make more mistakes. After three full days without water, your judgment is seriously impaired.

After a week you can be dead.

My problem was that even a sedentary person should drink at least two quarts a day. When you're in a heightened, traumatized state, as I was, your demands are far greater. I'd started off in Bosnia with only one quart of water, and it was going fast. That day I downed a four-ounce flexipak every hour or two; once I splurged and drained two within thirty minutes. I'd anticipate and savor each sip — it was mealtime for me. By the end of the day only three of the eight containers remained. I peered at the gray skies with more than usual interest, rooting for a deluge. When it came, though, it was only a sprinkle.

The day turtled along. That morning I'd heard the cows again, closer this time, and with the faint clang of a bell. They had a handler out there with them, I thought, maybe more than one. The Gazelle buzzed past again in the afternoon. I monitored on my radio when I could, as futilely as before; I wondered if it might be broken.

Late in the day, however, I made contact of another sort. It reminded me that survival was not merely a physical test, but a spiritual one, and that I needed to keep summoning all of my resources, from every dimension of my life.

I grew up in a strong Catholic home, Irish on my father's side, Italian on my mother's. I attended Catholic schools for several years, received communion and confirmation. I was raised to believe that a person's relationship with God was the most important part of one's life, and that one practiced one's faith by being a good person.

My faith was a very personal thing, and I didn't pretend to be the most devout person in the world. In the Air Force my churchgoing was erratic; when you keep our kind of work schedule, Sunday morning is sack time. And when I did go to church, I wouldn't deck myself out in a three-piece suit and sit in the front pew and make out that I was holier than anyone else. I'd sit in the back, in a T-shirt and jeans, and keep quiet. Much of the time I wouldn't even listen to the service; I'd be having a more private conversation.

The previous winter I'd returned to the States for training, and in March I went through an exercise in Las Vegas. One day

I visited two friends of my mom's there, Nick and Anita Sinaly. Our talk turned to Bosnia, and it turned out that Anita had been there. She'd visited the southern part of the country, a place called Medjugorje, where the Mother Mary had reportedly been sighted. Never much of a believer in miracles, I filed the story away.

But on the afternoon of my third day in Bosnia, I prayed to the Mother of Medjugorje. Before long I felt a definite presence. It grew more and more vivid, until I could *see* it, shimmering in my mind's eye. It's hard to put this into words, but I saw the vision through feeling it, and the feeling was very warm and good. That international chorus welled up again, praying for my safe return.

I can't tell you how important that vision was to me. It gave me the courage to go on.

I knew I had to move again. I was still too close to people, and the cowherd's bell was a real concern. In evasion you're constantly on the lookout for armed pursuers, but you also dread accidental contact with local civilians. With no plan or intention, someone walks into your position — or you into theirs — and bingo, you're confronted with a stranger who's as scared as you are and likely beyond your control.

My plan was to push on southeast, to reach a ridge en route to the big hill and give my radio a better shot. Getting there in one gulp would mean a longer trip, and that much more exposure. But I thought it was worth the trade-off: the farther I made it from the road, the safer I'd be. And I'd come to view the darkness as a personal friend of mine. By now I knew it better than anyone who might be chasing me.

After delaying till deep into the night, when even the trees seemed to sleep, I began the laborious process of getting out of my hole-up site. I stood up as before, in dozens of disconnected movements, pausing between each one.

I was getting good at this. It had become a sort of test — I wager I'd made myself, at table stakes — to not disturb a single twig.

I checked off the items of my survival gear, loaded them into the rucksack. I secured my radio in my vest pocket, with the earpiece plugged into my ear and ready for monitoring. I folded my tarp and netting and slid them between my vest and flight suit. After adding the two sections of my evasion chart, I looked five months pregnant. Strapping the rucksack to my back, I stepped out into the cul-de-sac and picked my hunchbacked way to the path and the maze.

The sky had cleared — easier to travel, easier to be spotted. I made out the Big Dipper and found the North Star, the most reliable navigating tool yet invented. As long as you didn't forget that the constellations shifted fifteen degrees per hour, it was hard to get too lost. I double-checked now and then with my compass, shielding its glowing dial with my hand before slipping it back into my vest pocket, always dial-side in. My mind worked double time on just that sort of minute detail, on all the trivial things that were now so important.

The effort in my legs told me I was going uphill. The vegetation thinned, and then my path broke into a field. I was at a crossroads. It would be dicey to move straight across, to bare my silhouette against the open ground. But there was no way I could circumnavigate the field along its shrubbed border; at my snail's pace, I wouldn't finish till after daybreak.

Audentes fortuna juvat, I thought to myself, and I walked out into the open, faster now, stopping for cover at the occasional bush. I was feeling good about my progress, charged by my foot speed, when I came over a rise and stopped short. A pair of gigantic power relay towers loomed before me, a quarter mile apart. What really bothered me was the antenna that stuck out from one of them; I wondered what it was receiving.

The first birds were stirring when the field narrowed back into a broad path, then up an embankment to denser foliage. Exhausted by a mile's march with a full pack, I found what looked to be a secluded cove. Its southern edge was bounded by a granite ledge, a steep slant of rock about six feet high, and it was at the base of this ledge, with a tree and some bushes around me, that I stopped to make camp.

According to my evasion chart, the dense hills of Bosnia were home to wild boars, bears, wolves, and European vipers, a first cousin to the rattlesnake and equally poisonous. But I never saw a ground animal till that early morning by the rock ledge, when I heard a rustling that startled me half to death. Then I spied it. A black squirrel, with all the trimmings: bushy hair, big tail, pointy ears. We eyed each other for a second or two, and then he scampered off.

The only other animals I'd come across were small, sparrowlike birds. More than once, while I'd lain motionless, I'd watched them perching on nearby branches or fluttering in the undergrowth three or four feet away. There were moments I longed for a hunting bow, but I never had a serious notion of killing a bird for food. I wasn't about to build

162

a roasting fire, and they were too quick to catch, in any case.

After two radio calls and a combat nap, I awoke with a start. Predawn light poured into the cove and told me that I'd landed in one nice, fat predicament. My immediate area was more sparsely wooded than I'd thought in the darkness. I'd be easily visible from within the cove. What's worse, the rock ledge I'd nestled up against would block a quick exit.

Once again I risked a daylit move. After warily approaching the edge of the cove, I dashed ten yards across it and into a thick clump of thistle bushes, getting scratched up in the process. I burrowed into the middle of them and bedded down. To better cover my body, I used the entire tarp, rather than doubling it up; I'd just have to take more care to keep the silver side under wraps. My concealment was fine now, and so was my vantage point — I could watch the whole cove and the path leading into it.

But once again there was a drawback. My feet, sticking out as usual, sat just three feet from the edge of the grass.

It was Monday, June 5, my fourth day in Bosnia, and it passed uneventfully. I heard the rumble of a jet high overhead, assumed it must be friendly, and tuned in to monitor on Guard and Alpha. I had a scare when the nipple of my earpiece turned up missing; my ability to monitor safely depended on a piece of plastic the size of a pinkie joint. I took a deep breath and began to rummage deliberately through my gear. Twenty minutes later I found it, inside the tarp.

As I lay on my side, the Beretta mashed into my ribs. I removed the gun from its holster — the barrel was already rusting, to my annoyance — and added it to the array fanned out beside me: radio, GPS (I'd rung in the satellites for a new set of coordinates), compass, and my wool and leather mittens, which I'd remove whenever I needed manual dexterity. I made continuous mental notes of where everything was in relation to my body. If I had to shove off in a hurry, I'd best not leave souvenirs.

Using my knife mirror, I could see that my cheek burns had scabbed over, with no apparent infection. I felt an occasional irritation when the nape of my neck rubbed against my collar, but I could live with that. I had only two real physical problems, but they were big ones: cold and thirst.

I was cold and damp every minute I spent in Bosnia. The days were gray and chill, and the nights worse. It got so bad before sunup that I'd expect to see frost on the grass. I had three thin layers on my torso — T-shirt, flight suit, vest — and they weren't enough to stop the shivers. By now I'd added the larger portion of my evasion chart to my makeshift bedroll; it lent some extra waterproofing, but it didn't keep me warm.

My water shortage, meanwhile, had dipped into the red zone. I'd drunk my last flexipak that day; my lips were chapped, my tongue a dry slab in my mouth. It had drizzled each afternoon, but just enough to keep my feet waterlogged.

I knew I was headed for physical trouble, and soon. The evasion chart showed no streams in a safe direction. While I assumed the cows must have a trough somewhere, near a farmhouse, I wasn't ready to take that kind of risk. I listened for frogs, which might have led me to a creek bed — no dice. I even thought about using my big survival knife — my Rambo knife, I called it — to dig down to the water table, but that seemed like a long shot at best.

I was left with one option, the one I'd come to trust most: I prayed. I closed my eyes and reached out for He who had yet to fail me. I prayed for a cloudburst, for a downpour, for the kind of rain that made Noah famous.

At some point that afternoon I fell into another restless sleep . . . and awoke to the sound of heavy hooves clomping down the path. The cows! They bore in closer and closer, into the cove, across to my thistle bushes — it felt like the whole world was crashing in on me. There were two of them, maybe more. They lowered their muzzles to the thick green grass and began chomping away, four feet from my boots.

Had they been drawn by the smell of me? I lay still as a stump — afraid to spook them, afraid to get stepped on. I could hear the bell of their handler, off in the middle distance. The last thing I wanted was to draw his attention.

Those cows ate and ate, and ate some more — never looking up, engrossed in their meal. To amuse myself, I gave them names: Alfred and Leroy. (I realized later that cows should have female names, but it didn't seem to matter at the time.) I christened their herder as Tinker Bell, after his infernal clanging.

Those cows stayed near me forever. If they didn't move on, I thought, it was just a matter of time before Tinker Bell would come in to get them. I felt like a party host with two incredibly obnoxious guests who refused to leave. Finally, after an hour's dinner, the animals lumbered off, restoring my privacy.

The weather shifted as on other days, with clouds building by late afternoon. Then I heard a far rumble, and my spirits perked up.

That evening it rained, a soaking thunderstorm that wouldn't stop. I received it like manna. Feeling less tense, knowing that the storm would discourage anyone chasing me, I set out the two ziplock bags that had contained my water packs. Still lying on my side, I propped them up in my nest, struggling to keep their mouths open to the pouring sky. It was nonstop work, and not too successful: whenever a drop spattered the top of the bag, it would flatten and shut on me.

Then I got another idea. I swiped my yellow sponge over my puddled rucksack, then squeezed it into a bag. The result was a gratifying stream of water; I could see the line of liquid rise within the ziplock. The rain that fell directly into the bags would be cleaner, and taste better, but that sponge was a lot more effective — that was where I made my money. I used it on my tarp, on my vest, on any leaf that held more than a drop or two.

When I finished, hours later, I'd added a pint to my travel pouch and a few ounces down my parched throat: another victory.

God had heard my call once more, and I prayed now to thank Him. I never stopped praying while I was in Bosnia, day and night. If I'd used a calling card to reach heaven that week, I'd have run up one whopper of a bill.

Hours later, with the weather front past me,

the night sky cleared, till there was hardly room for all the stars. I made out Venus, bigger and brighter than anything around it, and then two meteors streaked across, the most brilliant I'd ever seen. They reminded me of the skies at Camp Reed, in northeastern Washington, where I'd spent several summers in my youth. I felt a pang for that time in my life, when everything had seemed so much simpler.

Ever since I'd joined the Air Force, each home had been but a way station; I'd moved so often that I had boxes I never unpacked. Yet at that moment I wanted to get home so badly — to Aviano, to Alexandria, to Washington State. To all the folks I'd left behind.

I decided to stay put that night and make an all-out effort on the radio. Since my prior attempts had come up empty, I needed to try something different: a beacon, the all-purpose distress signal on the Guard channel. A beacon had greater range — up to a hundred miles — than voice transmissions. And it attracted the broadest possible audience, both military and civilian.

Of course, the bad guys had radios, too, and my pulse pounded in my ears as I nudged the radio switch into beacon mode. To avoid being traced, I left it there just a few seconds. I heard the distinctive sound, like a high-pitched car alarm, in my earpiece, and knew it was working. I monitored — first Guard, then Alpha, then Guard again. Nothing out there.

I waited ten minutes, then tried the beacon again. I monitored Guard for two minutes: blank static. I moved to Alpha: more of the same. I came back to Guard — and then the reception broke through, the first English I'd heard in four days. The voice was faint and garbled and breaking up, but it moved me more than a Garth Brooks medley, which is saying a lot. My excitement surged as I strained to make out the words: "Flashman, this is Magic on Guard . . . heard some beacons . . . see if you can —"

Then a second voice, equally faint, responded: *"Basher Five-Two, this is Flashman . . . hear me."*

He was talking to *me* — he was searching for me! I had no idea who Flashman was — a fighter pilot on temporary duty out of Aviano, maybe, or from some other base in Italy or France. But all that mattered was his next awesome call, which I read as clear as a bell: *"Basher Five-Two, this is Flashman on Guard, if you hear me."*

Barely stopping myself from screaming a reply, I spoke tight into the radio mike: "Flashman, this is Basher Five-Two."

"Basher Five-Two, this is Flashman, if you

hear me, on Guard."

He wasn't receiving me. I jumped back in: "Flashman, this is Basher Five-Two, how do you hear."

I waited — a minute, two, three. I'd lost him.

"Anybody, Basher Five-Two." But Flashman was gone, without learning that I was alive.

I'd be lying if I said I wasn't disappointed, to come so close to making contact and then to fall short. But that night had uplifted me nonetheless. My evasion movements had paid off; by reaching higher ground, I'd brought my radio into receiving range. And just hearing Flashman's voice made me feel reconnected. I wasn't out here on my own. I was still part of a big and loyal team.

Three touchstones got me through my time in Bosnia. The first was my faith in God, a trust repaid a thousandfold.

The second was my confidence in NATO and the U.S. armed forces, my certainty that they'd do all in their power to get me out. Magic and Flashman clearly hadn't given up on me; I could hardly pull the plug on them.

The third was my love for family and friends. I gazed back up at all the stars, the same stars they could see in Italy or Virginia or Seattle, and I wondered if my loved ones, too, had been able to keep the faith.

Stacy O'Grady was on a ladder when the news came. Her eighth-grade students had graduated the day before, and that night they'd be having the traditional dance. My sister was hanging decorations when one of her seventh-grade helpers approached and said, "Miss O'Grady, you have a telephone call." Stacy asked him to take a message, but three minutes later the student was back: "Miss O'Grady, it's your mother on the phone."

Stacy knew right there that something was terribly wrong — in our family, you didn't call on a workday afternoon unless it was an emergency. That was the way Stacy had learned of aunts' and uncles' deaths. *Who was it this time?* As she tore off the ladder and into the teachers' lounge, she thought of me, the person in her life who was never quite safe.

"Is it Scott?" she cried into the phone, and then she broke down. The conversation was impossible — Stacy was hysterical, and my mother could barely talk. Finally the message got through: "Scott's plane has been hit by a missile."

When she heard that, Stacy was sure I was dead — she couldn't fathom the possibility that I could survive such a thing. Her worst premonition had come to pass. For years she had thought that my life would end in a plane, had *felt* it coming. My sister had been born three years after me, to the day, and we had some unspoken connection.

She knew that some people would think this a heroic way to die. But to Stacy it was simply a waste, and she was livid with anger. She was angry because her children yet unborn would never know their uncle. She was angry that we'd spend no more Christmases together, that her birthday — *our* birthday — would always be filled with regret.

For five minutes she sat sobbing in the lounge, near the point of hyperventilating. Word spread among her colleagues, who wanted to do all they could, but there were times when grief left room for no one else. My sister wanted the whole world to go away.

Mom had told her my dad was alone, and Stacy knew she needed to be with him. Her boyfriend drove her to O'Hare, speeding down the emergency lane to get by Friday rush-hour traffic. On the way they heard a bulletin on National Public Radio: an F-16 pilot had been shot down. The fact that the pilot went unnamed — and would remain that way, to avoid leaks to the Bosnian Serbs —

made it worse. Made it surreal and disconnected, as if the pilot weren't really human.
Made Stacy want to scream, "That's my
brother you're talking about!"

In the plane she sat for two hours like a
stone, staring at the seat in front of her, waiting to land. When the cab dropped her at my
dad's house in Alexandria, she ran in to hold
him and be held, until she knew she wouldn't
crumple when she saw it in black and white.
Then she took the letter, the same one sent
to my mom, and read it five times; she feared
missing some hint, some clue. "We have to
keep our hopes up," my dad kept saying, but
even he didn't sound convinced.

Then they went to their rooms, to try fitfully
to sleep, hoping — and fearing — that the
morning would tell them what the letter could
not.

Up early, they channel-surfed the television,
but it was no use — there was nothing new.
They walked out into the pale light, down
the Fort Williams Parkway. On every lawn
or driveway they saw the *Washington Post,* its
front-page headline blaring. They'd walk by
people coming out to pick up their paper —
just a routine morning ritual — and Stacy
would think, *They have no idea.*

My brother, Paul, arrived from North Carolina that Saturday morning, and they heard

173

from Colonel Charles Wald, commander of the 31st Fighter Wing, who happened to be stateside for a training exercise. Now he'd be rushing back to Aviano; he gave my family a telephone authorization code to patch through to him, day or night.

That afternoon the first big news broke: the Bosnian Serbs were claiming they'd recovered me and were guaranteeing my safety. My family was euphoric — they could handle my being a hostage if it meant that I'd survived the shootdown. The U.N. hostages taken on the ground appeared to have been treated humanely. Besides, they assured themselves, I was worth more alive to my captors than dead.

Things were looking less tragic. My Uncle Tom, a senior inspector at the Drug Enforcement Administration, had an inside contact in Serbia, who also believed I'd been captured. Tom joined the family for dinner; a friend had dropped off a pork loin, and my dad brought up an Australian chardonnay from his wine cellar. "Scott would want us to celebrate," he said, and they did. The next twenty-four hours would surely bring some resolution.

On Sunday morning, Tom and Paul tried to relax with a hike along the Potomac, but Stacy wouldn't leave the house. She worried that they'd miss an important call, and she'd grown addicted to *Headline News,* which would be on in our den all day long.

Soon Stacy knew CNN's cycle as well as her name: world news, national, business, sports. The shootdown remained the top story, retold twice each hour, but as the day passed without developments, Stacy's mood sunk. The Bosnian Serbs had yet to produce evidence that they had me, and the experts were voicing doubts. Stacy just kept watching, with blank robot eyes, as they rehashed the story. The part she hated most was when they showed the charred remains of my F-16. While no cockpit could be seen, the wreckage spoke volumes about the violence that had crossed my path.

As the camera panned the plane, it zoomed in on my flight data recorder, an orange box with a prominent printed message:

FINDERS' INSTRUCTIONS
U.S. GOVERNMENT PROPERTY
IF FOUND, RETURN TO NEAREST
U.S. GOVT. OFFICE

With Tom and his energy gone, it was a bad night for all hands. Every so often someone would reel into a crying jag; there was no controlling it. They tried to prop one another up, to take turns being strong and avoid a collective meltdown.

They were learning the value of patience — they had no choice in the matter — but it was a hard way to learn.

Monday was the Day of the Beacon. The Air Force announced that they'd picked up an emergency beacon signal in the vicinity of the shootdown, giving new legs to the theory that I'd safely ejected. Stacy caught herself referring to me in the past tense, and the family made a pact: present tense only, from there on in. My dad — his spirits lifted by his close friend Margaret Jones — even started making plans for a family ski trip in Colorado. It was a time for positive thinking.

But when Stacy reached Colonel Richard Brenner, vice-commander of the 31st Fighter Wing, at home that evening — it was around 2:00 A.M. Aviano time — he could not confirm that the signal was mine, or even that it held much significance. A beacon might have any number of sources: a civilian distress call, an old crash site, a Bosnian Serb ruse. Without voice communication to back it up, it was totally inconclusive.

Hopes were dashed again. All the conflicting reports — from the Air Force, the media, the family's private contacts — were making them crazy. It was like a Ping-Pong match, Paul thought, or a jigsaw puzzle with half the pieces missing, where your own imagination had to fill in the holes.

By Tuesday the Bosnian Serbs had conceded that they'd lied — they didn't have me, after all. There was a new CNN report, a parachute sighting, that offered fresh encouragement. My father knew that I'd been well trained at Fort Benning. If I'd gotten out of the plane with a working chute, he felt sure that I'd have made it.

But Colonel Wald denied any knowledge of the parachute. Loath to raise false hope, he refused to give the family any speculative information. The military was doing all things possible, the colonel assured them, some of them secretly. My family trusted and believed him. My father called the colonel "a pain-killer," for his earnest, soothing manner. But hope was ebbing.

Defeated, Stacy called my mom. They considered that it might take weeks or months before they knew what had happened to me. And there were cases, they knew, where the families never found out. My mom had once dated a boy who'd gone to Vietnam and turned up missing in action. He stayed missing for more than twenty years, until they shipped his scant remains back to the United States.

How could you live with that? How could a parent — or a sister or a brother — go on?

My father had returned to work that day, to read a few radiographs and escape the house, and while he was there it helped some. But when he came home, it was worse than before. He felt hopeless and very old.

Stacy went out alone in the backyard and stared up at the sky. With no comfort to be drawn from any worldly source, she looked to something higher. *If he has his cross on,* she thought, *everything will be okay.*

CHAPTER SEVEN

It was still dark as ink Tuesday morning when I woke from a doze to an explosion that shook the ground and gave me the shock of my life. It sounded like incoming fire, no more than fifty yards west.

I hunkered down inside my tarp. My mind ran wild. Did they know where I was — or were they trying to ferret me out? Was it a mortar? A hand grenade?

It took me a while to get a grip — to realize that what I'd heard was not the landing of a shell, but perhaps an artillery recoil — or, from what I'd be told later, the sonic boom of a very low flying jet.

The night returned to normal. But that bizarre wake-up call, along with the visit of the cows the day before, convinced me to keep moving south and over the big hill. My hole-up site was a disaster waiting to happen. And even if I chanced to make radio contact here and transmit my coordinates, it was no place to stage a rescue mission.

But I wasn't going anywhere yet, not until the next night. I could tell by the birdcall that dawn was closing in. The sun would be up by five o'clock. Not that I was timing it; I'd scarcely looked at my watch of late, kept its shiny metal hidden under the sleeve of my flight suit.

The passage of time no longer held the same meaning for me. I marked the daily cycles — the low clouds rolling in at midmorning, the afternoon rains, the spotty gunfire in the distance just before sundown. But beyond those, time was a trivial item. My nights became days and my days became nights, since my main activities — movement and radio talk — were reserved for after dark. I had no sleep cycle to speak of; I was getting an hour or two per day in snatches. I had no office to show up at, no errands to run, no dinner dates to prepare for, no TV shows to look forward to. I had nothing better to do than to live. To survive. That was a full-time job and then some, and I did it one minute at a time.

On the other hand, I wasn't ignoring the passing of the days. I knew it was Tuesday, June 6, and that I was into my fifth day of evasion. I wasn't particularly hungry; a stomach shrinks fast when you put nothing in it. But I had to keep my strength up for that forty-five-day siege, if need be. I ate a few more leaves — the oval kind, not the hairy ones on the thistle bushes — and they weren't any tastier or moister than before. Then I saw an ant crawl by my head, and one of those cartoon lightbulbs went on inside.

I knew that most insects are edible. In much of the world, in fact, they are viewed as healthy taste treats: high in fat and salt, more protein than beef, chock full of vitamins and minerals. In Africa and Asia, where meat is unaffordable for many, the big beetles are especially popular — they're supposed to have a nutty flavor when roasted.

I went through Air Force survival training in winter, when the bugs were gone, and I'd never eaten so much as a termite. But now opportunity knocked, and I was on the prowl. The spiders and bees I'd come across didn't perk my appetite. Had I run into a cricket, I'd have peeled off its head and legs and wings, all the hard parts, and mucked it down. But the Bosnian crickets, though they raised a racket, stayed out of eyeshot.

Which left me with the ants.

They were good-sized bugs, with reddish heads and brown bodies, and I'd seen two or three of them crawl around me the day before. This time I followed the straggler's path. It developed that he was joining a feast two feet past my head, where about twenty of his friends were chowing down on a decaying worm. I watched for a while, lying on my left side, mulling my move — were they fire ants? would they sting me? — before reaching out with my mittened right hand. As soon as one of the ants crawled on the mitten, I squished it between my fist and my rucksack.

Making sure it was dead, I took off my mitten, picked it up with my fingers, and — here went nothing — popped it whole into my mouth. There are honey ants so sweet that children cry for them for dessert, but this guy was sour as lemon. I waited two minutes for a reaction, then crunched him up and swallowed.

After that we were off to the races. My first kill had set off the alarm, and the remaining ants were running every which way. That made them more difficult to trap, but I got the hang of it. I became a squishing machine. Within a half hour I'd thrown down fifteen of them.

I didn't experience the least bit of food aversion; I'd have eaten a plateful if it had been served to me. There isn't much bulk to an ant, and the episode was worth more in entertainment than nutrition. It was one of my rare mental breaks.

And I can't deny that it was nice to be the

hunter for a change.

I heard a jet again that afternoon and monitored my radio when I could, but nothing came through. Later on I made out the report of a far helicopter and the cracking boom that had shocked me, now well off to the east.

With a few hours left till sunset, I prepped for my night move. For maximum concealment, I applied some green and brown camo paste to my face. The ski mask was still valuable — you lose 70 percent of your body heat through an uncovered head — but its hole had sagged, till it drooped below my mouth. The camo — and my growing beard — would prevent my skin tone from betraying me.

Then I heard a familiar, heavy clomping down the path and a clanging bell behind it. It was Leroy and Alfred, and this time they'd brought along their pal, Tinker Bell. *A fine job of hiding you've done,* I told myself. *You picked the cows' favorite dining spot.*

I buried my face into the tarp, too fearful to peek out, hoping against hope that the cows would pass me by this time. But I'd have no such luck — it was like a nightmare I couldn't shake. Leroy and Alfred were creatures of habit. They cut across the cove the same way, barreled straight toward my thistle patch, stopped two yards from my feet. Their noise was the same; it felt like it came at me from 360 degrees. Their table manners were just as gross — the word "grazing" didn't do justice to that sloppy hubbub they made.

I couldn't believe it. I'd somehow survived a supersonic missile, a last-ditch ejection, a parachute ride from higher than the top of Mount McKinley, and several platoons of rifle-toting paramilitaries. And now I might be defeated by a pair of stupid cows.

If that wasn't enough to tick me off, there was Tinker Bell, ding-donging like a maniac on the opposite side of the cove. At a hundred feet, that bell was a killer. The only thing worse than hearing it ring was hearing it occasionally stop; I'd imagine that Tinker Bell had spotted me and taken off to get his buddies. But the bell never stopped clanging for long.

I thought about what I might do if the herder confronted me. Run for the hills? That sounded right. Overpower him if he got in my way? I could try, though I didn't feel up to two falls out of three. Use the Beretta? Bad idea — the shot would bring people in from all around, and they wouldn't be feeling kindly toward me.

Please, God, don't let him find me. Keep me safe until sundown, till I can find my way out.

After a half hour's snack, Leroy and Alfred

crashed off — out of the cove, down the path, with Tinker Bell hot behind them. Why they left was a mystery, but I knew that the next time I saw a cow it had better be on a plate, medium rare.

Hours after dark, when the land had settled, I packed up my gear and left the thistle patch. I got tripped up more than once moving out of that thicket, nearly fell on my face. I stepped on more dead branches in thirty minutes than I had in four days. But I made it out.

I was on the watch for a dirt path that might have channeled an artillery piece and the soldiers to man it — that was a path I didn't want to cross. I moved along small, flat fields, bordered by bushy trees — sometimes east, sometimes south, wherever the terrain took me. A ripe moon half lit my way, and the Big Dipper was out again, but my zigzagging got me disoriented, even with my compass out. I tried to get references off the big hill, now visible to the south, but there was more than one hill out there, and it was hard to correlate what I saw with what I recalled from my evasion chart.

I felt like I'd been let out of a closet and into a strange, dark house.

How many nights would I be stumbling along like this? How far would I have to go to be rescued? I didn't let the questions hang: as long as it took. I had to be willing to walk back to Croatia if need be — through mountain passes and cities and enemy forces. It might take me a year or two, but I could do it.

Anxious to see if Flashman or someone else was up there, I monitored on Guard as I moved. But when I used the earpiece, my inner ear would magnify the sound of my own breathing, masking the sounds around me — a dangerous proposition. I took out the earpiece and turned the radio off.

Creeping through the shadows, I moved onto a game path forged by people or cows. I came upon a series of stone walls, no more than three feet high, and clambered over them. The vegetation thickened. I neared a large stand of trees, where my path became two, circling round in either direction. I was pondering which branch to take when I heard a small splash and felt my ripped right boot fill with water; I'd stepped in a muddy puddle. Muttering a silent oath, I slogged on to the left, and it was then I made my first glaring error in judgment since deserting my hit-and-run kit at my landing site.

By that point I'd depleted my water again. There'd been no rain to speak of since the thunderstorm. I'd tried sponging up dew, but it was hardly worth the effort. I'd kept a mouthful or two of water in the travel pouch in reserve, for morale's sake, but I hadn't drunk any all day long.

It would have been easy enough to submerge the pouch in the puddle, then purify the muddy water later on with iodine tablets from my survival vest. It just slipped my mind. I was mad about my wet boot and preoccupied about where I was headed.

I had a new strategy for my next hole-up site. Rather than keep moving till dawn, I'd stop an hour or more before sunrise, leaving me time to scout out the best spot and feel more secure. The time came as I reached another short stone fence, running north to south. To its east I could see the lighter grays of open pastures. On the west side, where I was, there were lots of young trees and bushes. It seemed logical that any cows would graze on the open side; they weren't likely to hurdle a wall.

I settled on a sheltered spot a hundred feet from the fence — the kind of place, I thought, where a guy might bring his lady for a picnic in the woods. I broke off some more branches for extra concealment and placed a leafy one over my feet.

It felt like I'd trekked over three time zones since that first pell-mell dash, fresh from the parachute. In fact, I'd traveled less than two miles from my landing site.

By the time I bedded down, it was too light to try transmitting; that would wait one more day. According to SAR procedures, after all, it was up to NATO to initiate the radio call; the more often I called in the clear, the greater my risk of detection. As before, I would limit myself to monitoring until well after dark.

As eager as I was for rescue, I stayed patient. I felt I'd have just one shot, and I was going to do it right. No matter how slowly the hours dragged by, a week of evasion — or a month, or more — wasn't much of a sacrifice. Not when you weighed it against the chance of captivity, when the clocks could stop for years, or for good.

While this third hole-up site was my best yet, the new digs were less than deluxe. I spent the first part of that morning excavating softball-sized rocks that dug into my side, and the rest of it managing my camouflage. There were lots of dead low branches on the near trees, and they'd disintegrate at the lightest touch.

Other than that, I was happy with my new address. I could hear cows and people beyond the stone fence, but no closer. I had wearied of company, and it looked like I'd left it behind.

I'd never been much of a camper, even as a kid. The mosquitoes liked me too much, for one thing. (A great blessing in Bosnia was the absence of biting insects.) Whenever I spent a night in the wild, I was always glad to retreat to a cabin with a real bathroom. Now, after five days in the great outdoors, I felt filthy. I'd have done bodily harm for a shower. I'd have paid a year's salary to brush my teeth — they felt like they had socks on.

The worst was the cold. I'd been shivering on and off for a while, and now my body was shaking. I kept wishing for sun, if only to lay out my socks to dry, but the skies weren't cooperating. My boots were full of water — they felt as wet as my mouth felt dry. I'd planned to wait till dark to remove them, but by early evening I couldn't stand it anymore; I had to air those boots out. I pulled them off, then peeled away my soaked, yellowing socks. I inspected my feet for frostbite; I'd had frostbite once at the age of twelve, when my chairlift stalled on a ski slope, and now I checked for the telltale white patches. None were visible — a big relief. But my toes were shriveled like raisins, and almost numb. I tried to warm them with my wool mittens.

Then I did something I never would have believed one week before. I took those wet woolen socks and wrung them out into a zip-

189

lock bag. The water was rusty brown, about the color of mushroom soup, and there was less than an ounce of it. The flavor was even worse than you'd expect, but I was *thirsty,* and my small drink encouraged me.

I would keep making my way, by any means available.

I lapsed into a combat nap . . . and into one of those dreams born from wanting something so bad that your subconscious constructs it. I dreamt that it was okay to come out of hiding — that a safe recovery point had been prearranged with the United Nations. That the local farmers were sympathetic Muslims. That I could give myself up to the next person I saw and he'd get me dinner and a bed. That someone would pick me up the next day and drive me out of the war —

It was just a five-minute mental vacation, a break from the grind of evasion, but I pulled myself awake to cut it off.

I checked my tarp, my netting, the branches that cloaked me, and resumed my wait for the dark.

Some six years before, while awaiting the start of my pilot training, I tried to raise a little money as a flight instructor at Spokane International Airport. Students were hard to find, but I got hired by a land survey outfit to fly grids for an aerial photographer.

I moved in with the Ewings, some longtime family friends. Their son Greg was living in Seattle, so I stayed in his bedroom. Once I woke up at two in the morning and knew I wasn't alone. There was a presence in the room. An incredibly powerful presence — an evil presence. It was a web of hatred and deceit and connivery. It was darker than the night; it was a moral blackhole. I wasn't afraid. Somehow I knew that the presence wasn't out to harm me. It aimed for something more despicable — to entice me, to *recruit* me. It was as if I had to make a choice, then and there, as to which path my life would take.

It wasn't a hard choice. "Jesus Christ is my Lord," I prayed, "and I denounce evil and all its doings."

The presence vanished, like a gust of foul wind. I'd never felt it again until the day I landed in Bosnia, when it was amplified and everywhere, near and far and in between. I recognized it immediately and felt it each day I was there. It stood for all the horrors of war — for the hospital bombings, the "ethnic cleansings," the torture of mothers whose children were gone.

Once I began praying, I realized that two wars were being waged here: the human, political war, the one that had burst its dike and engulfed me, and a spiritual war, that age-old battle between good and evil.

As mighty as the evil was here, I felt the good was stronger still.

There's a lot of eye-for-an-eye business in old-time religion. They paint God in fire and brimstone, as a fury to be feared.

But that isn't the God I experienced in Bosnia. The God who came to me stands for pure love and goodness. He won't force you to accept Him; you must take that first step. All you have to do is open your heart to Him, and you've grasped the whole meaning of life: forgiveness, utter and complete.

Forgiveness is so hard for us on earth. It doesn't come naturally — we learn it through prayer and faith. By my second day in Bosnia, I'd already forgiven the people who'd shot me down. We were all warriors, all doing what we thought was right. For me to hate the people who launched that missile would have hurt me worse than the SA-6 did. It would have burned me in places where salves and surgeons couldn't penetrate.

In Bosnia I caught just a glimpse of God's love, and it was the most incredible experience of my life. I'd tapped into the brightest, most joyous feeling; I felt warmed by an everlasting flame. For all my physical complaints, I'd been on a spiritual high since that missile and I intersected.

At around midnight, growing confident that no one would discover me, I turned back one corner of my tarp, exposing the shiny, silver side. I'd be moving out to try my radio, and I wanted to make sure I could find my way back. Though I wasn't assuming I'd be rescued that night, I'd be on the prowl for a suitable LZ — a landing zone for a helicopter to park on.

Just outside my hole-up site, I stopped dead and stared. Two dead tree trunks — skinny and stunted, no more than six feet tall — stood crossed like a giant "X." I hadn't noticed them coming in. Had someone picked up my trail and snuck up to plant the trunks for a marker while I slept? Had that been the case, I was ready to nix my game plan, grab all my stuff, and head for the hills. But when I stooped down to investigate, I found the dead trees to be normally rooted. I exhaled and moved on.

I walked in a straight line along the edge of the woods, slightly uphill, staying west of the stone fence. Every few steps I'd stop, look, and listen. I'd glance back to my hole-up site, then break off a branch and place it down in clear view, till I'd formed a dotted line to my bed. The branches would come in handy for added camouflage the next day.

My journey would be short that night, but hunger struck me en route. I reached down and grabbed a few blades of grass; if it suited Alfred and Leroy, it should be good enough for me. It tasted like a bad salad without the vinaigrette, but I was glad to have something in my mouth.

As I walked and chomped, I reviewed the facts. It looked like no one had heard my voice transmissions. But Magic had made out my beacon, and so they might now suspect I was alive. It was my job to confirm that suspicion, and the surest way to do it would be to put out another beacon, and hang the risk.

After fifty yards I reached a small, circular clearing, just right for the radio. The moon was full, brighter than I might have liked, halfway up the horizon to the south. Moving to the clearing's center, I took out my GPS receiver to get a hack for some new coordinates. I quickly rang up *four* satellites — a good omen, I thought — and brought them up again to double-check.

It was time to set off the beacon, but I hesitated. Was this really the soundest way to go? Was I getting reckless, impatient? I returned to the edge of the clearing, sat down on a rock, and clicked the radio on to monitor through my earpiece. I picked a few more blades of grass and had a chew, more for nerves than appetite.

I was like the kid on the edge of the diving board for the first time; he's not sure it's such a hot idea, but he's gone too far to turn back. I couldn't just monitor indefinitely and drain my batteries — I had to go for it. I retraced my three steps out to the open. I came up hard on the beacon on Guard, longer than before.

Retreating to my rock, I prayed that someone had heard me. I pushed the radio's switch one stop to monitor on Guard. Then another stop for Alpha. Then one more round for each.

White noise each time. As dead and depressing as all the other static before Flashman had entered my life.

Feeling stubborn, I walked out there again, tried another beacon. Went back to the rock and listened for a few minutes. Ate some more grass. Waited some more before taking it from the top.

Please, Lord, let them find me tonight. At least let them know I'm alive.

It became a Bosnian cha-cha: beacon, pray, monitor, sit, wait. I went through it three or four or five times — I lost count, to tell you the truth. It wasn't till after 2:00 A.M., when I'd been at the clearing for over an hour, that someone cut in on my dance.

As I monitored on Alpha, I heard three distinct clicks on my radio — the sound a live microphone makes on the other end.

The sound a live *person* makes.

The news got to Captain Thomas Oren "T.O." Hanford within half an hour of the shootdown. As weapons and tactics officer for the 510th Fighter Squadron in Aviano, Hanford was leading a routine briefing for his squadron mates on the afternoon of Friday, June 2. He was interrupted by the ops officer, who broke into the room with a grim-faced bulletin: "The Triple Nickel has lost somebody. We don't know who it is, but we think he might have gotten shot down."

An hour or so later, as the pilots and their wives gathered for a long-planned squadron party, the squadron commander called them all into the mass briefing room. "Captain Scott O'Grady has apparently been shot down by a surface-to-air missile," he announced. "His whereabouts are unknown."

The party was canceled, of course. Like any group of expatriates, the 31st Fighter Wing was a tight-knit community. You'd find a spirited rivalry between its two squadrons, the 510th and the 555th, but there were also many strong friendships. A lost pilot was like a death in the family. And in a way it was more jarring still because every officer in that briefing room knew that what had happened over Bosnia could as easily have happened to him. Each one of them was chained to the luck of the draw.

As people milled numbly about the squadron, Hanford met up with a shaken Wilbur Wright and learned nothing to make him feel better. Wright had watched my airplane come apart, my flaming cockpit tumble into the clouds. He'd seen neither an ejection nor a parachute; he'd heard neither beacon nor voice up on Guard. It didn't look, he told Hanford, like anyone could have survived.

A broad-shouldered, second-generation Air Force fighter pilot, with a classic flattop haircut and a rambunctious sense of humor, Hanford knew the score. He was thirty-three years old, had flown F-16s for seven of them, and he'd lost at least fifteen pals and squadron mates along the way. The first time was the worst, when Hanford's best friend in the world, a super talent named Josh Levin, ran into the side of a mountain during an exercise in the Philippines. It happened on Valentine's Day 1989, and for days afterward Hanford would sit and stare, neither eating nor sleeping. What was he supposed to do now?

He was supposed to press on, to keep doing the job he'd been trained for. Over the years he grew familiar with the drill — the solemn announcement, the common grief, the broken families. But he never got used to it. In all that time, Hanford had yet to hear a happy ending to any of these stories; once a pilot was downed and missing, it was only a matter of time before they brought back the pieces. Still, you didn't want to give up on someone, to admit he was truly *gone,* till that body came back. Hanford wouldn't give up on me, but he was skeptical, to say the least.

That weekend the glum pilots at Aviano kept pressing their intel shops for updates. A number of beacon signals were judged to be spurious; they were spread way out, and none were close to the F-16's crash site. When the Bosnian Serbs released videotape of the wrecked plane on Saturday, the pilots pored over the pictures, searching for signs of the ACES-II seat or the parachute. Finding none, they couldn't be sure if that was good news or bad. They simply had no evidence what-soever to pin their hopes on.

When the Bosnian Serbs claimed they'd captured the man they'd shot down, the pilots were willing to believe it, as I had fallen into an extremely hostile area. Hanford just hoped I wasn't being abused. Two days later, when it was clear that they *didn't* have me, Hanford saw two possibilities. The first was that the

Bosnian Serbs had killed me and wanted to dispose of my body without anyone learning of it. The second scenario — and this one seemed less likely — was that I was still on the loose and evading.

In the aftermath of the shootdown, NATO had severely curtailed Deny Flight missions. With high uncertainty over the location of the Bosnian Serb SAM rings, few aircraft were being allowed to go "feet dry" over Bosnia itself; those that did were packaged with a web of other planes for protection. With the 510th taking over Deny Flight from the Triple Nickel that week, Hanford had flown "feet wet" on Monday, staying out over the Adriatic, off the Croatian coast. His cap lay two hundred miles southwest of the crash site, so far off that he didn't even try to radio me.

On Wednesday, June 7, Hanford was "fragged" again as flight lead for a feet-wet Deny Flight mission. This time, however, he'd be patrolling more to the north, about seventy-five miles west of the crash site. With his wingman, Clark Highstrete, in a ten-mile trail, Hanford reached his cap at 11:00 P.M. and flew his regular racetrack ovals at 25,000 feet. On his "hot legs," when he was headed toward Bosnia, he'd train his radar on the no-fly zone. Throughout he stayed in touch with Magic, NATO's early warning platform, to learn of any violators the F-16s might have missed.

The sky was quiet that night. Every now and again Magic would repeat, "Picture clear," meaning its radar screens were clean. Even so, Hanford's job wouldn't permit him to transmit to me; other jets had been deployed on search-and-rescue sorties over the past five days, and the two missions were kept distinct.

That changed at 1:25 A.M. on Thursday, June 8, when Magic told Hanford and Highstrete that they were "clear to RTB," or return to base. Hanford almost did just that, but he still had six thousand pounds of fuel, about forty minutes' worth beyond what he needed to return to Aviano. Much later, when he finally got home to his wife, he'd explain that he would have felt foolish crawling into a nice, warm bed, knowing that "my bud down on the ground" was a lot less comfortable.

He'd also been swayed by some rising confidence at the squadron intel shop. Over the last day or so, they'd become less pessimistic about the chance that I was still alive. Hanford didn't know all the details, but he knew enough to make him ambitious.

"We have twenty more minutes of play time," he told Magic. "I'm going to stay out here and monitor SAR Alpha."

"Roger," Magic agreed, and added some encouragement: "You're clear to call out on it if you want."

At that point Hanford was more or less at liberty. Leaving Highstrete to monitor Magic's frequency, he switched his own primary radio to the Alpha channel used on June 2, the one I would be using still; he'd jotted the frequency numbers on the lineup card on his knee board, just in case.

Hanford also turned off the squelch function on his radio, filling his headset with a constant shout of static. The pilots normally left the squelch on, to tune out cabdrivers and rock stations and save themselves a headache. With squelch off, Hanford would hear all of those low-power sources — and just maybe a handheld radio in the wooded hills to the east.

Still in a racetrack pattern, Hanford called out in his deep baritone, "This is Basher One-One, looking for Basher Five-Two."

He squinted his eyes and strained to listen, to get inside the nagging static, the way he used to listen as a boy alone in the dark.

After a minute he tried again, keying his mike to transmit by lifting a lever on the throttle with his index finger.

"This is Basher One-One, looking for Basher Five-Two."

Hanford held no particular expectation of hearing anything back — no real confidence that I was still alive, for that matter. Even in the best case, he thought he was probably out of range of my handheld radio, though he knew its range expanded at night.

But all that was secondary. Hanford figured he owed me this much. He'd keep trying.

At around 1:40 A.M. the static on Hanford's headset turned irregular, lapsed into a surging rhythm — a rough echo, perhaps, of my beacon signal on Guard.

At that moment, Hanford had no firm idea of what he was hearing — only that there might be *someone* out there.

Highstrete checked in on their interflight radio — the twenty minutes were up, and Magic wanted to know when they'd be heading back. "We got twenty more minutes of play time," Hanford told the NATO aircraft. His fuel gauge had just passed "joker," a level he set at a thousand pounds above what he'd need to get back. It was the point where a flight lead began looking to gather the horses for home.

"Okay, roger," Magic replied. There was no immediate replacement scheduled for Hanford's two-ship, no urgent need for the planes; if the man had the fuel and the patience to stay out there, there was no cause to overrule him.

Hanford kept putting out his call, once a minute, but his static had reverted to its first flat roar. As he sped through the moonlit night, he could see scattered pinpricks of light in the Bosnian hills. His own lights were shut down, save for his console controls. For ten seconds at a time Hanford shut his eyes tight — Highstrete was stacking 2,000 feet above him, and they were too high to run into anyone else — and strained his ears even harder.

At 2:00 A.M. Magic queried them once again. Hanford got annoyed and said firmly, "Magic, we're going to stay out here and we'll let you know when we're returning to base." He'd made his point: stop bothering us.

Hanford was fast dipping toward "bingo" fuel, or 3,500 pounds, the amount he'd reserved for his return. He'd made the calculation conservatively, with some margin of error. Experience had taught him to be more cautious on night flights, when you were more prone to miss a landing and might need a second approach. But some intuition made him push the envelope that night. One good thing was that Highstrete had five hundred pounds more fuel than he did; it was a cardinal sin for a flight lead to run his wingman out of gas.

At 2:06 A.M., while pointing toward Bosnia on his hot leg, Hanford recited his call for the umpteenth time: "Basher Five-Two, this is Basher One-One on Alpha." He felt dispirited, as though he were just going through the motions. In a few minutes he'd have to give the search up.

Then he heard something behind the wall of static, so faint that he might have imagined it: *"Basher One-One . . . Basher Five-Two."* The voice sounded feeble, lethargic, but Hanford wasn't jumping to conclusions. His first thought was that another pilot must be transmitting on Alpha — maybe a search-and-rescue guy who wouldn't be pleased with Hanford's horning in on him.

"This is Basher One-One," Hanford said, enunciating with extra care. "I can barely hear you — say your call sign."

Once again he just did hear it: *"Basher One-One . . . Basher Five-Two."*

With his hot leg ending, Hanford altered his cap orbit from an oval to a circle less than ten miles in diameter, to reduce his time out of range. As he turned away from the coast, he lost all audio reception, but forty-five seconds later, about 270 degrees into his circle, he began to pick it up again. *"Basher Five-Two . . ."*

Hanford was still unsure. "Understand you are Basher Five-Two. This is Basher One-One on Alpha."

"Bingo, bingo," the on-board computer pealed in its programmed soprano. Hanford ignored the warning. He'd pushed his circle to the east, in an effort to improve his reception, until he was feet dry over the edge of coastal Croatia and not far from a known SAM ring. Highstrete urged his flight lead to turn back, and Hanford ignored him, too. The weary voice kept breaking up into static, but Hanford was a stubborn fisherman, determined to reel it in.

"Basher Five-Two, this is Basher One-One, say again," he pleaded.

And then he heard it, really *heard* it, still weak and parched-sounding, but now familiar and definitely there: *"This is Basher Five-Two, read you loud and clear."*

Hanford felt lifted in his seat: "Basher One-One has you loud and clear!"

But then the F-16 turned west, and the voice receded — it was like missing the brass ring on the carousel and having to wait till you came round again. Sure enough, as Hanford circled back to the east, the voice returned, even stronger: *"This is Basher Five-Two, how do you hear?"*

"Basher Five-Two," Hanford boomed out, "this is Basher One-One!"

"I'm alive, I'm alive!"

"Copy that!" Hanford said. He could feel

the tears forming. Though he knew who it was, Hanford needed some authentication to get the rescue ball rolling and to ensure that no one would be heading into a Bosnian Serb ambush. He needed to ask for something no outsider would know — some fact I would never reveal in captivity. Hanford had served at Kunsan Air Base, with the Pantons, and he knew my history there.

"What was your squadron in Korea?" Hanford said.

"*Juvats — Juvats!*"

"Copy that, you're *alive*! Good to hear your voice!" This was less than standard radio discipline, but Hanford was literally shaking with emotion. He struggled to regain some control; it was hard to fly an F-16 with tears streaming down your face.

"*I can't believe this is happening,*" Hanford said to himself. "*I can't believe he is alive.*"

CHAPTER EIGHT

I never recognized T.O. Hanford's voice that night — my radio was too weak. But I knew from his call sign that he was an F-16 pilot from Aviano, and I knew he was out to get me home. When we made contact, I got goose bumps; every hair on my body stood at attention. My mouth was so dry I could scarcely talk, but I wanted to laugh, scream, cry, all at the same time. It was the purest rush of energy I'd felt in my life.

I felt like I'd been born again.

Once Basher One-One had affirmed who I was, he took down my GPS coordinates. At first he had trouble translating what I'd given him. But then he remembered the letter code he'd gotten from his squadron's intel shop — the same code I'd given to Wilbur in that unusually thorough SAR briefing before our flight.

I knew that I had a chance to get out that morning. The two conditions were satisfied:

I was definitely alive, and a pickup point was established. (Unwilling to rely on written markings in his dark cockpit, my finder would mark my spot by using his pen to punch a hole in his map.) A recovery mission would now hinge on time and timing, on good luck, and — not least — on faith.

Before he left to refuel, Basher One-One directed me to turn off my radio and save my batteries — sound advice, as communication would be vital in the actual rescue. He told me to come back up on Alpha at the half hour; he'd find some other platform to get in touch with me then.

Still tingling, I returned to my rock at the edge of the clearing. At 2:30 I checked in with a pilot call-signed Ghost, who verified my identity through a more formal NATO protocol. Fifteen minutes later Basher One-One was back on my freq. I was glad to hear his voice again — he'd be my emotional anchor as long as he stayed out there — but the message he brought was dismaying.

First he asked my condition. I told him I was okay, though as I said it, a small, nameless chill went through me.

Then he dropped his bombshell: "Magic wants me to pass you the word, *mañana*."

Tomorrow. NATO wanted to wait till the following night! To *leave* me here another day.

I punched the button on my radio and blurted, "No, get me the heck out of here *now!*" The sound of my own voice startled me. It was the loudest I'd heard it in quite a while; I might have lost control for a moment there.

Basher One-One tried to soothe me: "Copy that, hold on." He went off to get more information and returned seconds later: "There's a lot going on. They're waking everybody up right now. Shut off your radio and come back in half an hour. If you have an emergency, I'll always be monitoring this channel."

I'm a less than patient person in the best of times, and that next thirty minutes would drag like the worst soap opera in the history of the world. As I sat on my rock, my head filled with pointless speculation. Had I blown it by telling them I was all right — had it dulled their hurry to retrieve me? If I were hemorrhaging out here, they wouldn't think twice.

And then, as I looked at it more rationally, I knew I'd had to speak the truth. We were professionals; we depended on one another's objectivity. The men in charge would do all in their power to save me, just as I would for them.

I knew that the specially trained rescue teams liked to work in the dark, when they'd run less risk of exposure and their night-vision equipment lent them an edge.

I also knew that NATO would be putting a significant package together, from various bases — a lot more than one or two helicopters. It took time to coordinate that kind of operation, and dawn crept only two hours away.

My head knew all of that, but my heart — and my instinct for self-preservation, at a fine edge after the last six days — told me to pay it no heed. All that radio talk had compromised my security; it wasn't stretching it to believe that the Bosnian Serbs were homing in on my whereabouts. If I had to, I'd go back to my hole-up site. But in my heart that chapter had closed. They *had* to pick me up this morning. The alternative — holding on for another long, waterless day in a less than secure hiding place — was too unpleasant to consider.

I stepped breathlessly back into the clearing at 3:15 A.M., but Basher One-One had nothing new. At 3:30 it was more of the same, though he tried to keep me busy: "Stay hidden, and get ready to mark," he advised. "You *will* be rescued."

I felt more and more frustrated. It didn't help that our reception was erratic, and we'd keep having to repeat things. My life depended on those garbled messages, on my draining batteries; I worried that the coming daylight might put Basher One-One out of radio range.

At 3:45 I could hear *his* discouragement. I knew he'd been turning the heat up on Magic, who was linked to NATO's Combined Air Operations Center in Vicenza. But if a final decision had been made, it had yet to filter down to us. With a pomegranate of a lump in my throat, I said, "Understand they're going to pick me up tomorrow?"

Even through the static Basher One-One could hear how forlorn I felt. "The whole world's behind you," he said, sounding choked up himself. "NATO's behind you, and the U.N., and every plane in the world is going to be taking off to come get you. We're working on it. They're going to get you — just hang tight."

We agreed that I would come up again at 4:15.

The birds were out, and first light was close behind. I lay down behind a small mound of dirt among the trees, to find what concealment I could. We'd reached a decision point, I thought; it was time for NATO to either fish or cut bait. If I couldn't get a confirmation on the next call, I'd tell Basher One-One I was through — that I'd hide out the rest of the day and would reestablish contact the next night.

Anxious to bring things to a head, I came out into the clearing five minutes early, at 4:10 A.M., and waited for my call. This time Basher One-One had news, and I could tell it was good by the glow in his voice. "They're rounding up the boys right now," he told me. "The assets are airborne. Everything's scrambled — they're throwing everything they have at you. It's only a matter of time."

The cavalry was coming, after all.

"Get yourself in a good position," Basher One-One continued, "and just hang tight. Do not let your batteries run out — stay off the radio if you have to."

I clicked my mike to acknowledge, both to save my batteries and to draw less notice from any Bosnian Serb interlopers. I wouldn't speak again till it was absolutely necessary.

Lying back down behind the dirt mound, I could hardly contain myself. I had to stay focused on the tasks ahead of me; it was way too soon to celebrate. There were still a thousand things that could go wrong — and if I needed any reminder, the volume knob on my radio chose that moment to pop off. As the knob also controlled the set's on-off function, its loss would be disastrous. I raked the grass and recovered it.

As the gray dawn lit my new neighborhood, I saw that the clearing was too small to accommodate a helicopter. At best, a chopper might be able to hover and lower a line to hoist me up. I surely didn't want to move elsewhere and risk capture. From the sounds of the day before, I knew there were people close by.

That dark thought stayed with me. The closer I got to being rescued, the more I thought about getting caught. I loaded a round in the Beretta's chamber, took the pistol out of safety, and returned it to the holster on my left side. The Lord knew I wouldn't relish any gunplay, but I wasn't about to go gently at this stage of the game.

If anyone tried to stop me, I'd treat him for what he was: a threat to my life.

Now that the operation was launched, I had my own second thoughts. All too soon the herders would be up and around; we wouldn't be a secret for long. The night before, I'd heard some shooting off to the south, and I prayed that my rescuers wouldn't become targets. My skin was dear to me, but I didn't want to save it at another's expense.

The conditions weren't helping. The sky had been planetarium-clear while we'd waited for NATO's decision, but now a low cloud deck was forming at 2,000 feet. A ground fog began to roll in around me. If it got much worse, a chopper landing might be out of the question.

Basher One-One shared my concern. At our next call he asked, "How's the weather in your area? If you can see blue sky, click the mike twice."

It took some hunting, but I managed to find a chink of blue, and gave two clicks. It wasn't a beach day, for sure, but I knew that Bosnian weather was volatile, and I prayed it might change for the better.

At 5:00 A.M. Basher One-One called in for the last time, just before moving out to refuel. He said he'd be handing me off to a new flight lead, Rock Four-One, who would take on the mantle of on-scene commander, my liaison to NATO forces.

At the tanker Basher One-One would tell Magic he wanted to stay on the case. But he'd been out there six hours, and that was enough. "We know he's your bud," Magic told him, "but they want you to go home." He reluctantly banked northwest toward Aviano, his job well done.

When Rock Four-One came up at 5:15, I guessed who he was: Vaughn Littlejohn, another pilot with the 510th. His call sign was apt: Littlejohn was as steady as they came, a guy you'd want to take to war with you.

He and his wingman, Scott Zobrist, would pick up Hanford's coastal cap and keep it warm for the duration.

Hearing Littlejohn was like a long-distance call from a friend you thought you'd lost touch with. It summoned back in a rush the life I'd mislaid in Italy.

"Some of the rescue assets are airborne," Littlejohn reported. "Conserve that battery power, and be ready for authentication. We're here for you, we're going to get you out."

This was *real*, I thought. My friends were out there, and they were bound to get me home.

I wondered where the helicopter would take me. To Croatia, where U.N. forces had a coastal airfield? Or, if its range allowed, all the way to Italy? I was ready to be flexible. If ever there was a journey that meant more than the destination, this was it.

At that point I was monitoring the radio full-time. Littlejohn guided me into the homestretch. At 5:45 he checked in with his final update and a magical word: "The package is *inbound*. Stay up on your radio and listen up. They should be over your position in the next ten or fifteen minutes."

I felt wrung out and lit up at the same time, like a boxer ahead on points going into the last round.

By 6:00 A.M. I heard the distinctive blast of a pair of F/A-18 Hornets. They were coming low and coming fast, streaking straight at me, and — best of all — they belonged to the U.S. Marines. Their role was to confirm my coordinates for the package to come. The first one buzzed nearly over my head, though still above the low cloud deck and out of sight. The second made contact, asked me to give him a mark as he passed. Facing south, I heard him just off to my right, and yelled out, "Mark! Mark!"

The pilot said, "Confirm we flew right over your position."

"You're to the northwest," I corrected, "maybe half a mile."

So far, everything was on the money.

The clouds were gradually breaking up, the chinks of blue bleeding into small patches. The ground fog had thinned and stalled on my downhill side. I was on the edge of the mist — close enough for some cover, but not shrouded from the recovery forces. It looked like God was giving me one more gift.

At around 6:35 A.M. the Hornet passed me the word: "They're coming in real soon. Stand by."

It might have been two minutes later when I heard it: a vague thumping at first, off to the southeast, but quickly building into the hollow, choppy sound of a rotor. I jumped into the clearing and tried to vector the helicopter into my position, holding the compass from its back end and screaming reference headings into my radio. When my earpiece fell out of my ear, I didn't bother reconnecting it; we were past the whispering stage.

Then I heard the pilot — "Basher Five-Two, this is Bolt, come in, over" — and two Marine Cobra attack ships broke over the horizon. I could see them through a hole in the ground fog. But could they see me? "Pop smoke," Bolt ordered. I was already ahead of him. I felt for the nubby tip of my flare canister — the opposite end was a sparkler for night signals — and pulled off its cap, then cracked off the seal to ignite it. I knew it would work when I heard the pop, like the sound of a .22. Pointing the canister down at a forty-five-degree angle, so the dripping phosphorus wouldn't burn me, I watched the red smoke pierce the fogbank and waft up into a billowing haze.

Within twenty seconds, as the flare stopped puffing, the Cobras circled closer.

"Directly overhead!" I cried.

"We see you," Bolt said.

I warned him about the shots I'd heard south of me the night before, and then I made ready. Just minutes before I'd been doing my best to blend into the landscape, but visibility was now a virtue. I plopped my orange hat atop my ski cap; though useless in hiding, the hat now seemed the perfect touch. Any rescuer would know that only an American would wear something as dumb as that.

When the smoke dissipated, I popped my second flare. I looked up longingly at the Cobras, wished they'd lower me a rope and close the deal. For that matter, I'd have grabbed onto one of their skids if it could get me home. I didn't yet realize that these guys were there as the muscle, as advance men to secure the area for the transports to follow.

Seconds later, one of the Cobras dropped some yellow smoke just to the south of me, and then I saw the two hulking Super Stallions, swooping down in single file and behind some near trees.

"I'm off to your right!" I shouted.

"Did you see the CH-53s?" Bolt demanded. His name, I'd learn later, was Major Scott Mykleby; he wasn't a man to fool around. I struggled to remember what those particular choppers were called, but drew a blank.

"I see, uh . . . I see . . . the big helicopters. I'm off to their right."

"Move *towards* them."

"Copy that," I said; Bolt didn't have to tell me twice. In survival training they teach you to stay put and let rescue forces come to you. But I wasn't inclined to hang around, like some commuter at a train station — I wanted to get this show on the road. I found a dirt path that plunged into the forest, in the general direction of the helicopters, and I took off.

With the pistol in my right hand and the radio in my left, my flares and compass still tethered to my vest and flopping with each stride, I wasn't exactly poetry in motion — at one point I tripped and fell on my face. I was going for broke now, all caution behind me. I ripped past foliage like some crazy-legged tailback, dashed down that zigzag path as if it were a guantlet.

"Keep going towards them, Basher, keep going towards them," Bolt spurred me. "They're looking for you."

"I'm going," I huffed, "as fast . . . as I can."

This wasn't any cinch, not yet. My rescue was awaiting me — I could hear those idling choppers — but they weren't handing out free passes in the Bosnian woods that day. They'd sent a rescue helicopter to within spitting distance of Lance Sijan before North Vietnamese machine guns repelled it; Sijan never got another chance.

Two hundred yards later, my lungs burning, I broke through a tree line and some lingering fog, and there they were, rotors spinning, settled on a sloping, rock-strewn field. The area was dotted with trees and stumps and bushes — not exactly your textbook landing zone.

I'd had limited experience with helicopters and had never felt real comfortable around them, but those Super Stallions looked pretty good to me. The Cobras swung above us, their guns primed; higher still circled a pair of Harrier jump jets, like protective mother eagles.

From one of the choppers, off to my left, a dozen or more Marines had fanned out to secure the field's perimeter. The second Stallion had redone its landing after setting down against a log, and now lay dead ahead, just fifty yards away. I ran a few steps into the field, then stopped for permission to advance. Which helicopter was I supposed to board? How would I get on without a rotor decapitating me?

So I stood there — dying to move, halted by doubt, and generally overwhelmed by what was happening. I stood there until I saw a burly young sergeant just outside the right gunner's hatch of the near chopper. He was waving me in — waving me home.

I pumped ahead in a beeline, still clutching my gun and my radio. They tell you *never* to run at a helicopter with a loaded gun, but I wanted the Beretta handy. I wasn't on the chopper yet, and even after I got there I wouldn't be home free. If the helicopter got shot down, a definite possibility, I wanted to be able to defend myself.

But when Sergeant Scott Pfister took stock of the apparition staggering at him — a bearded, wild-eyed man in a mud-caked flight suit and a grotesque orange hat — he decided it might be safer all around to disarm me. Pfister met me a few steps from the doorway and rapped my right wrist with his forearm. The Beretta dropped harmlessly to the grass; the sergeant retrieved it and put it away. My hat, dislodged in the scuffle, would be the only material evidence of what had happened here this morning.

"I'm gonna get you on this aircraft," Pfister told me. He boosted me up and through the hatch, past a .50-caliber machine gun. Another pair of arms — I'd find out they belonged to Colonel Martin Berndt — pulled me through and inside.

Forget about the cavalry; I'll take the Marines any day.

After my trusty Swiss Army knife sliced off the tethers at my vest — they'd entangled some webbing in the aircraft — I fell in a heap on a sling bench that ran the length of the left wall. I tried to say what I was feeling toward those courageous men around me.

There were no words big enough, so I settled for two small ones:

"Thank you, thank you, thank you . . ."

I could never overstate the skill and valor of the sixty-one people on those four choppers, the ones who plucked me out of my nightmare. But in fairness, those helicopters were but the tip of a long and mighty spear. They were just one part of a well-planned, flawlessly executed mission that involved more than forty aircraft, hundreds of troops, and some of our top military minds.

Looking back, the stage for my rescue was set several days before my shootdown. As tensions in Bosnia rose with the bombing in Pale and the wholesale hostage-taking of U.N. peacekeepers, the 24th Marine Expeditionary Unit was recalled to the Adriatic from an exercise in Sardinia.

The regiment-sized 24th was no stranger to risk or pressure. It had been devastated in Beirut in 1983, when a suicide truck bomber blew up its barracks and killed 241 men in the unit. It had launched dramatic missions in the Persian Gulf, northern Iraq, and Haiti. One of its higher-profile teams, deployed on an amphibious assault ship named the USS *Kearsarge*, was a forty-two-member TRAP force: Tactical Recovery Aircraft and Personnel. The platoon had recently made a name for itself in Somalia by bringing back three helicopters after forced landings.

On June 2, shortly after the missile found my F-16, the TRAP team was "stood up," by Colonel Berndt, the 24th's commanding officer. For the next six days it would remain on round-the-clock alert status. The Super Stallions were readied on the *Kearsarge* flight deck; the men ate and slept with their gear within reach.

They weren't the only ones working to get me back. NATO officers at the CAOC in Vicenza slept on cots by their communications consoles. French and British jets flew low-level recon over Bosnia, with fighter and radar-jamming aircraft along for protection. The Pentagon threw out a Priority One intel net, including spy satellites that could see through clouds.

Meanwhile, the men in charge had to sift through a barrel of red herrings. At one point early on, Slobodan Milosevic, the Serbian president, assured the U.S. State Department that I was alive and that the military commander in Bosnia had been ordered to usher me safely to Belgrade. The following day, a spurious beacon signal set off a wave of conjecture.

But no one could move until my fate and

whereabouts were established. As days passed, more than a few people doubted I was ever coming back — and who could blame them?

At the CAOC, frustrated fighter unit reps lobbied for more aggressive search-and-rescue efforts. The generals and colonels countered that more was going on than the captains knew about. CAOC faced a catch-22. They needed radio evidence to confirm that I was alive, but the surest way to get that evidence — to fly intensively over suspected SAM rings — would put other pilots' lives at risk.

On the early morning of June 8, Berndt was up late, working in his stateroom, his radio tuned to Alpha. When he heard Basher One-One's excitement — my own transmissions were too weak to be audible — Berndt sensed that this was the real deal. A half hour later he took a call from London. Admiral Leighton "Snuffy" Smith, the NATO commander for southern Europe, was placing the 24th on ready-to-launch status.

At 3:37 A.M. the two men talked again, and Berndt said the TRAP force could be ready to roll within an hour. That assurance leap-frogged the *Kearsarge* group over a special operations force in Brindisi, the admiral's primary SAR option; based on the boot of Italy, the Brindisi team might have needed up to four hours to reach Bosnia. (After the operation was over, Admiral Smith would offer a simple explanation for his choice of the 24th: "They were there and they were ready.")

Though others pushed to wait till after the following nightfall, Berndt wouldn't flinch. The Marines could get the job done in daylight, he insisted, if NATO kicked in additional air support.

Even as I sweated out the verdict and prepared to take *mañana* for an answer, the people making the decision — Admiral Smith, Colonel Berndt, and Lieutenant General Mike Ryan, U.S. Air Force commander for southern Europe — never wavered.

At 4:39 A.M. Bosnia time, the order was official. The Marines had the ball.

As Admiral Smith put it, they'd decided that I'd "been there long enough, and we were willing to hang out a little bit, so we went after him."

To that bold decision I would owe my life.

The Marines hit their flight deck running. As the *Kearsarge* closed on the Croatian coast, they grouped in the hangar bay for final briefings. They test-fired their M-16s, rolled camouflage paste on their skin. They practiced Serbo-Croatian phrases that might come in handy: *"Stani! Pusti oruzja dolje!"* ("Stop! Drop your weapons!"). When Admiral Smith gave the green light at 4:39, they hustled up the ramp to board their aircraft.

Their average age: nineteen.

The TRAP team of riflemen and reconnaissance scouts would be bolstered by a tactical air control party, electronic warfare specialists, a communications group, medics, and a translator. In the best Marine tradition, the mission would be led by Colonel Berndt, Lieutenant Colonel Chris Gunther, and Sergeant Major Angel Castro, Jr., the 24th's highest-ranking enlisted man. The top men would stand by their most exposed troops.

At 5:05 A.M., one minute before sunrise, the TRAP force lifted off the *Kearsarge*, followed closely by the two Cobra gunships. In the lead Stallion cockpit sat Major Bill Tarbutton, once a pilot for President Reagan. No one envied him his present task. He'd have to pick his circuitous way over ridgelines and through narrow gorges — tough to fly through, easy to ambush. He'd be skirting at least two active SAM rings along the way, and those were just the threats that he *knew* about.

The Marines were eighty-seven miles west of me, closer than New York and Philadelphia, but they were headed for a moon shot's worth of adventure.

For close to forty minutes the choppers circled near the *Kearsarge*, waiting for their air support armada to come on-line. It was a formidable package, one of the largest put together since the Gulf War: F-16 and F-15 fighters; the tank-killing A-10 Warthogs; the Marine F/A-18 Hornets, with antiradiation missiles to take out any SA-6s; EF-111 Aardvarks and EA-6 Prowlers, to jam hostile radars and thwart them from locking onto the helicopters. To meet the planes' fuel needs, eight flying tankers were dispatched to the northern Adriatic.

By 5:42 all assets were screaming into the sun, with NATO's Airborne Early Warning on board to vector them to me. At around the same time, a backup set of planes and helicopters took off to monitor from offshore and assist as needed. Contingency reinforcements included a company-sized package called Bald Eagle. Were anything to go wrong, no one would be left hanging.

At 5:49 the TRAP force went feet dry over Croatia. With the Cobras two hundred yards in front of him, Tarbutton skimmed over the fogbanks, using them for cover. At 6:03 the Harriers took off from the *Kearsarge* and quickly caught up.

Krajanian Serb radar activity was detected at 6:21; the other side was watching and ready.

Ten miles from my position, the Cobras pushed out in front of the Super Stallions, to safeguard the way and scout for a landing zone. At 6:40 Major Mykleby, the lead Cobra pilot — the one who'd directed me to pop my flare — told Tarbutton to "Buster": come as quick as he could. Ground visibility was almost nil, but then Tarbutton saw a hole in the fog. He dove for it, with the second Stallion right behind him.

I was glad I'd taken the initiative and made my move toward the choppers; had I waited for the Marines to seek me out, we might have been stuck there too long. As it was, we sat for a nervous few minutes until all were present and accounted for in the other helicopter.

While we waited, Colonel Berndt shed his camouflage Gore-Tex jacket, and Sergeant Major Castro — a brawny, take-charge guy from the Bronx — slid me into it, full-bird colonel's rank and all, and snapped the buttons down the front.

Castro asked me if I needed a medic, and I shook my head. He handed me his canteen and I downed a quart of water in maybe five gulps.

I hadn't thought much about food to that point, but when Castro asked if I was hungry, it seemed like a very good idea. The sergeant ripped the top off an MRE (a Meal Ready-to-Eat), and lunch was served: chicken stew. It was cold and thick, like chocolate pudding — and I thought it was delicious. I wolfed three spoonfuls before my stomach closed for business; it had shrunk since I'd left my diner's paradise in Italy.

My lap belt strapped, my immediate needs sated, I wanted to let loose. I wanted to cheer, to give vent to my relief. But the evader inside me wouldn't let go. I was still in survival mode. I knew better than anyone how treacherous Bosnian airspace could be.

I would have happily talked to someone. After that much time alone, I was ready to talk about anything. But there didn't seem to be much interest in chatter just then. I did get to answer one quick question before we left the ground: How was I feeling?

"I'm good — but I'm ready to get the heck out of here," and by 6:48 A.M., six minutes after touching down, the choppers were aloft.

Five days and fifteen hours after landing in Bosnia, unannounced and uninvited, I had my return ticket.

As our Super Stallion soared up over a ridgeline, pedal to the metal, I looked at the faces staring wide-eyed back at me. There were close to thirty Marines inside that chopper. They were well trained and well armed, a group of confident young men, but this morning they seemed subdued behind their camouflage paint. It was the closest that some of them had come to combat.

They had good cause for concern. The mist was already burning off the hilltops. We'd be wide open to anyone with a spare bullet and a nasty attitude.

I was sitting near the gunner's door, with the chill air whistling around me. Castro directed two of the Marines to sit close on either side, then draped a thin tarp — a twin to the one I'd left at my last hole-up site — over the front of me. My shivering slowly subsided.

I'd needed some taking care of just then, and this sergeant knew just what to do.

With some fog cover still beneath us, the first half of our trip went without incident. The trouble began when we broke out over a clear valley. Castro, who was sitting on some ammo boxes between the two benches, leaned toward me and said something about "taking fire." I thought he was asking me about my time on the ground; it's really noisy in an open helicopter, especially when it's racing at close to 200 miles per hour.

"Yeah, I took fire," I said.

Castro raised his voice and shouted, "No,

we're taking fire now!"

In fact, we'd strayed into a Krajanian Serb light show. From below, you could see the orange muzzle flash of antiaircraft artillery; through the air came the corkscrew white plumes of the "man-pad" SA-7s, the shoulder-launched surface-to-air missiles. They fired at least two or three of them; one darted just below us.

The Bosnian Serbs had seen their trophy snatched out from under them, but they weren't conceding without a protest.

Tarbutton ducked "down in the weeds," as he'd later describe it, and my chopper followed suit, a mere fifty feet above the ground. It was a rough ride. We were moving as low and as fast as we could, hugging the roofs of barns and houses, bumping up to avoid strings of power lines, a helicopter's worst enemy.

But not quite low or fast enough. One round tore through Tarbutton's main rotor; a second struck one of our tail rotor blades. A third ripped through our cabin from back to front; it bounced off the roof, and then it got Castro in the back. The sergeant jerked around as if he'd been punched. A young Marine across from me reached down and picked up the spent round. The bullet had mashed into Castro's canteen — the one he'd replaced in his web gear after I'd taken my drink. Unfazed, the sergeant motioned the younger man to keep it.

Manning the gunner's hatch, Pfister replied with a burst of machine-gun fire. I wished I still had my own gun in my holster, though there was nothing I could have done with it.

The Cobras, guns bristling, were all out to protect us from the rear. But a Super Stallion is seventy feet long, a fat target. Our best offense was defense; we needed Godspeed to break free of this vipers' den.

I learned later that Radovan Karadzic, the Bosnian Serb leader, claimed to have sent orders "not to interfere" with my rescue — to respect it as "a humanitarian mission."

Someone on the ground apparently never got that message.

The Marines' faces were stone cold, tight as a miser's purse. I knew how they felt — I knew what it was like to lose control of your fate. *Please, God,* I prayed, *let none of these good men get hurt. Let us all make it home again.*

I flashed back to my first day in the woods, when I was sport for the men with guns, when every pore of my being aimed toward one goal: to survive. I ran through all the different scenarios that might grow out of this chopper ride — all the outcomes and risks and how I might respond, a thousand different permutations. I was prepared to get shot down in that helicopter, to crawl out of the wreckage, to evade and escape and live on. I could never, ever let go of that outlook, not till I was truly out of danger.

But to be honest, the feeling wasn't quite the same for me now. I was alert, make no mistake; I still took nothing for granted. But I somehow *knew* that no one in the Super Stallion would be hurt. As missiles and bullets traced the sky around us, it was almost as if I had to *make* myself feel scared.

Maybe I'd been through too much to conceive of dying at the brink of deliverance. Maybe fear no longer worked on me as it had a week before. I'd poured out so much adrenaline in the past six days that I might have built a tolerance to the stuff.

After five minutes the assault stopped, as suddenly as it had started. By 7:15 we'd left Bosnian airspace. We were kissed by warm air and the smell of the sea . . . and then I saw the beaches of Croatia and the clear blue water beyond them. It was one of the most glorious coastlines in the world, a blessing to my eyes.

As we went feet wet, my benchmates broke out in smiles and quiet cheers. They were clearing their weapons, running through safety checks. Someone placed a bulky life vest around me. I gave a thumbs-up sign to Colonel Berndt. I might have felt relieved, just a little.

But even then I was still surviving, still watching for the next cosmic banana peel. I was doing that over the Adriatic, and I was still doing it when my helicopter landed on the USS *Kearsarge*, at 7:29 A.M., to a raucous reception.

With not a single man hurt, the TRAP force had pulled off a miracle. I think my sister, Stacy, put it best, in her letter to thank them. The rescue mission, she wrote, was "one moment of perfection in a world of imperfection."

I felt the joy of that miracle as the Super Stallion touched down. Unhooking my lap belt, I stood and moved toward the door. A Marine squeezed the back of my neck with his hand. "Good to have you back," he said, his face shining.

Hopping onto the ship's deck, I broke into a big grin and a brisk trot, with Colonel Berndt's jacket hood flopping behind my head. A bunch of cameras were clicking at me — the first media onslaught — but I didn't stop to pose. I marched straight through a doorway, as directed, and into a crowd of happy, buzzing people. I shook the first hand I could find; it belonged to some Navy lieutenant.

It's hard to describe how I felt — it was as close as I'd ever come to flying without a plane.

But even then I was still on guard — still *surviving* — until after I'd been hustled into an elevator with a team of doctors. Only when I reached a ship's hospital bed, to be prepped for a grueling physical, did the last of my defenses tumble.

Now it was over, I thought.

Now I had my life back.

CHAPTER NINE

"I can't feel any hurt anywhere," I told Paul Rocerito, the naval flight surgeon who'd taken charge of me in the *Kearsarge* hospital. It was amazing; I felt like I was eighteen years old after a ten-hour sleep.

I changed into a hospital gown, and the medical staff had at me. They scrubbed me down, put in an IV, cleaned my burns, and gave me a shot in each thigh for parasites. They stuck in a thermometer and took out a blood sample, checked my blood pressure and heart rate.

They laid a big, rubber heating blanket over me to bring up my temperature; I'd checked in at 95.2 degrees Fahrenheit. Within forty minutes my temperature was back up to normal, and by that time I felt like an old man who'd fallen down two flights of stairs. As my adrenaline ebbed, I had aches and pains in muscles I'd forgotten were there. My red and swollen feet were killing me.

Rocerito's diagnosis: moderate dehydration; mild hypothermia; second-degree burns on my cheeks and neck, without any apparent infection; multiple scrapes and bruises, mostly on my fingers and knees; elevated blood pressure and a pulse rate of 110 beats per minute.

My most troublesome condition was a case of trench foot, more properly known as immersion foot, the result of prolonged exposure to damp and cold. Another day or two in the woods might have brought me trouble in walking, but there'd be no lasting damage. For now they'd try to lower the swelling by keeping my feet elevated.

After six days of trauma and virtual fasting, I'd dropped twenty-five pounds and now weighed in at around 135. I was skinny but not anorexic; I still had a little gut on me. Over the weeks to come I'd gain some of it back, of course, but not all — I kind of liked my new body. Call it the Scott O'Grady Escape & Evasion Diet.

Rocerito didn't want me eating till my urine cleared, and it would take four IVs to get there. After a while I put on a bathrobe and moved into a private room, for some rest in a bunkbed — to the extent you can rest with people poking and probing you every hour or so.

Later that afternoon I was debriefed for a few minutes by the Marines' intel. At 5:30 I took a shower — a peak moment, I can assure you. But I held off on the razor. Not shaving is a luxury for me, and I knew my bearded hours were numbered.

A string of visitors filed through: first the helicopter and Harrier jet pilots, the men who'd chanced all to get me home; then my wing and squadron commanders, who'd kept my family afloat.

It was an honor to see every one of those men, but the visitor who moved me the most — and stayed the longest — was the ship's chaplain. I told him what an incredible spiritual awakening I'd had in Bosnia and how God had kept me going. We prayed together, and I wept.

At 8:30 that evening they patched through a call to me upstairs, in the captain's cabin. I shuffled up there in my white USS *Kearsarge* robe and slippers, eager to talk with my family.

It turned out to be someone else: my commander in chief.

"The country was on pins and needles," President Clinton said, "but you knew what you were doing. The whole country is elated."

I told him what I'd tell others many times

in days to come: that the real heroes were my rescuers. "Mr. President," I concluded, "I just want to say one thing: the United States is the greatest country in the world. God bless America."

"Amen," the president said.

I stayed on in the cabin to talk to my family, and now my tears flowed freely. More than anyone else, they had shared my ordeal; now they were the ones who could best share my joy. I remember the feelings more than the words, except for one classic mother-son exchange:

"How are you?" I asked my mom.

"I'm fine," she shot back, "how are *you?*"

I went back to my room and finally got the green light for chow. There were three messes aboard the *Kearsarge* — one for enlisted men, one for senior enlisted, one for officers — and Bones, the med tech attending me, said the choice was mine.

"Just get me something from the enlisted mess," I told him. I wasn't disappointed; that night I feasted on crab legs and strawberry ice cream. They get good food on the ship. They deserve it, too.

One of my best friends from the Triple Nickel, Captain Miles "Quatro" DeMayo, brought me a new Air Force flight suit for the next morning. But my hosts had beaten him to the punch; in the corner of my room they'd hung a Navy flight suit with a USS *Kearsarge* honorary-member name tag. They'd even found a pair of flight boots, just my size. I lost count of the gifts I received on that ship, but one stood out: a patch of Snoopy, the comic-strip character, in his World War I flying ace regalia. It bore a simple message: "Be Humble."

The patch was normally reserved for sailors and Marines who'd rescued downed aircrew members. The guy who gave it to me had helped save a seriously injured crewman.

Since no one actually brought me to the Super Stallion, I had technically rescued myself, and so he passed the patch on to me. He said I was the first person in the Air Force to receive it.

I hoped I'd be the final owner of that patch — that no one else would need this kind of saving.

By the time Basher One-One began combing the airwaves for me, the O'Grady household in Alexandria was numb and exhausted. Too many hopes had been raised and dashed, too many hot theories shot down. My dad had lost eighteen pounds and carried his low-grade despair like a fever. Stacy and Paul didn't know what to do anymore. There were only so many walks and bike rides you could take.

It had reached the point where it hardly helped to talk, for everything had been said. Everything but the one monstrous thought that all of them shared, but none dared say aloud. Even later, in our happy-ending phase, William O'Grady choked on the words when he finally confessed them to a TV interviewer:

"I thought he was dead."

For the people who loved me most, it was time to settle in for what could be a long siege — to recover some semblance of normalcy, get some emotional rest. Paul would be heading back to North Carolina and his summer job the next day. With Dad back at work, Stacy couldn't see hanging on at the house by herself; she'd fly out to Seattle on Friday, to stay with Mom.

After a game of Parcheesi, the three of them had dinner and some wine, which made Stacy feel sadder. She trailed off to bed by 8:30, curling up with one of my childhood teddy bears.

My dad was the last to turn in, shortly after eleven. He'd barely slept when his bedside phone roused him. Like most doctors, he was used to late-night calls. He didn't assume anything special was up; he figured it might be his brother with some new rumor to chew on.

As he snatched up the phone in the dark, he glanced at his dresser, toward the digital clock with the bright red numbers. It was 12:48 in the morning, eastern time.

And this is what my dad heard: "Dr. O'Grady, this is Chuck Wald. Scott's alive, and the rescue team is going in now to pick him up. I'll call you back as soon as we know he's safe."

"He's alive," my father repeated after he'd hung up. "He's *alive!*" He ran down the hall and stood over my sister's bed: "He's alive, and they're going in to get him!"

Relief washing over her, Stacy reached up and held my dad close. It was as if, she'd say later, she'd tapped into pure oxygen after suffocating for six days.

The two of them ran into Paul's room and jumped on top of him. They trampolined in his bed, slap happy with joy, loudly rooting the Marines on to get me. It was like Christmas and V-J Day rolled into one.

They shuttled to an upstairs sitting room and clicked on the TV, where they heard the news repeated. My father warned that they couldn't know if I was safe yet, but it was hard to hedge their emotions. They were ready to give in — to surrender unconditionally to gladness.

In fact, Colonel Wald hadn't called till I was inside the Super Stallion. Fifteen minutes later, General Ryan made it official. "Your son is safe and inbound for the ship," he told my father. "Everything is fine."

Now there were two things to do: spread the news to our closest friends and relatives, and wait for the military operators to patch me through. At 1:30 the phone rang again, and three O'Gradys converged on it. But they didn't find me on the other end, not yet; they had to settle for the White House and a round of congratulations from President Clinton.

After a series of minor updates, CNN brought something new: the reel of my hopping out onto the *Kearsarge*, all smiles. My dad was encouraged by the pep in my step — he said it looked like I'd "taken a walk in the park and forgotten to shave."

By 3:30 in the morning their patience was fraying. My family didn't know it yet — the curtains were still drawn — but they weren't alone. A vanguard of reporters, with TV cameras and satellite dishes in tow, had already taken up shop on the street by my dad's house. Before long the driveway would contain a babble of impromptu press conferences, and Ted Koppel — *Ted Koppel!* — would be setting up his studio in the living room.

But the next ten minutes, after Stacy picked up the office phone downstairs, would belong to just the four of us. "Put him through — put him through!" she shrieked. They got on the speaker, all jabbering at once; for a while there I could hardly get a word in. Which was just as well, since I couldn't stop crying.

I told them my burns were minor, that I'd been through a lot worse. Then someone cracked a joke about my wrecked BMW and the nine lives I once had.

"I guess I've used up about eight of them now," I said.

"When are you coming home?" my father asked. If I'd ever wished for a ride on that *Star Trek* transporter, that was the time — there was no place I'd rather have been.

Across the continent in Seattle, Mary Lou Scardapane had done as well as she could to hold together — as well as a mother could do when her eldest child was sinking into a pit, beyond her arms' reach. She'd clasped onto every slim reassurance, layered them to her like armor: the beacon reports, the sighting of the chute, the still-missing cockpit. She'd heard the story of Colonel Roger Locker, another member of the Triple Nickel, who'd eluded capture for twenty-three days in Vietnam. *Twenty-three days,* she thought dully, and at first it sounded like one of those numbers too large to grasp, like the speed of light. But then she was heartened by the tale: the colonel had been rescued.

My mom became expert at reading between the lines or into the military's vague assurances. "Your boy is down there, and we're going to go get him," Colonel Brenner, my wing's vice-commander, had told her.

"You have valid hope," the Air Force chaplain counseled. "Hold on to it, Mary Lou. Wrap yourself in it like a blanket. It is your best friend."

It might well be, my mom considered, that these men knew more than they could let on — that they were toeing an intelligence tightrope. It might be that they knew I was alive but couldn't quite yet confirm it.

She'd opened her world atlas to the former Yugoslavia, tried to pinpoint where I'd gone down. She could see roads in the area, and water, and farmland. There were people out there — people who could help as well as harm me.

That atlas never went back to the bookshelf; my mom kept it spread out on a dining table. She'd touch the page, imagine I was there, and feel comforted.

But the nights were hard; to go to bed felt

like deserting a watch. And the mornings, when she'd awaken with the same stale thought — *We didn't hear anything* — were harder still.

On Wednesday night, before ten o'clock Pacific time, the call came in to my mom's husband, Joseph. She could tell it was important and sat on the floor by his chair, gripping his knees. Then she felt a rush go through his body and saw the thrill in his face. "Yes, yes," he said. He hung up and sat there transfixed.

"What is it, who was it, tell me who it *was*," my mom pleaded.

"That was Colonel Wald," Joseph said dreamily. "They have made contact with Scott. They are going in to get him."

At that moment, my mom would say later, "Everything fell apart inside of me." She collapsed to the floor, sobbing hysterically. She made Joseph repeat the news eight or ten times.

Then General Ryan called with the clincher, which my mom heard firsthand, and she took to screaming before the poor man could finish.

The events of that night, Joseph said, left footprints on the ceiling.

On the *Kearsarge* I thought I would sleep

like the dead, but you might say I was slightly overstimulated. I'd always stayed away from pills — I wouldn't even take aspirin for headaches — but deep into the night I accepted two Benadryls to calm me down.

After that I sagged into slumber. When I awoke, four hours later, I thought I was in my bed in Montereale Val Cellina. *Boy, what a nightmare.*

"Rise and shine, sir! Chow is ready." A cheery Navy Corpsman had come armed with a French-toast breakfast.

It was all real, from the missile to the *Kearsarge*, every last, unbelievable minute of it.

The doctors marched in with a new battery of tests, and I went up to get my back X-rayed. Almost everything was coming back normal: my liver function, my blood pressure, my heart rate (down to 96), my urinalysis. The swelling in my feet was down. I was running a mild fever, about 100 degrees — a passing aftereffect from my dehydration and hypothermia. I was weak and tired, and I couldn't walk too fast, but otherwise I felt fine.

I debriefed some more with the intel guys, then met with Admiral Smith, one of the nicer men I've come across in the military. We discussed the decisions that were made, on his end and mine, and how it all wound up fitting together.

I was back in my room, just hanging out, when Bones and Quatro DeMayo burst in, all excited: "Geez, you beat out O. J. Simpson in the news!"

"What the heck are you guys talking about?" I still hadn't grasped what was happening. I'd never expected to become the latest hot news phenomenon.

After a ship's tour and lunch with the ship's captain, Quatro helped me gather my gear. I'd have loved to stay on the *Kearsarge* another day or two — I'd never been treated better — but I was well enough to move out.

It was time to go home.

We'd be flown to the Italian coast in a Super Stallion, then switch to a Lear jet for the last leg to Aviano. My traveling party included Quatro, my doctor, and General Ryan. Both pilots were guys I knew from Ramstein; I was in good hands.

As I took leave of my hosts at the *Kearsarge*, there were some proud and happy Marines on that deck. These men were truly valiant. They weren't the glazed-eye action heroes from some Sylvester Stallone movie. They'd known what they'd risked to save me, and they'd been brave enough to face it.

I gave them a final wave and got on the helicopter.

★ ★ ★

On the first leg of our trip, fighting to be heard over the chopper's din, Quatro looked at me and held up three fingers. Then he grabbed his ring finger and yelled something out. I tried to follow his lips; it took me a couple repeats to get it.

The word he was shouting was "circus."

He was warning me about what lay in wait: a three-ring circus.

In the Lear jet, where you could actually converse, General Ryan elaborated. "You probably don't understand what you're in for, and you can do all of it, or none of it, or anything in between," he said. "Just take it as you go."

That's what I'd try to do, from there on out — but still I was utterly unprepared for my reception in Aviano.

More than five hundred people had gathered to greet me at the hangar, from MPs in blue berets to civilian wives in Bermuda shorts to babies waving flags from their strollers. There were magnums of champagne and a monster cake decorated with Old Glory. A group of schoolchildren held high a yellow banner, our national color of waiting. And above all the clamor you could hear a recorded Neil Diamond belting out "America."

I was, to put it mildly, overwhelmed. Thankfully my wing commander got me into a car, to a little reception hut they have for VIPs flying through the area. Bob Wright was awaiting me there, just as he had in our squadron building one week — and a lifetime — before. So was T.O. Hanford, and for a moment I wondered why. Then it dawned on me.

"You were Basher One-One," I said slowly, and the big guy nodded.

Let's just say we had a deeper friendship than when I'd left.

After changing into my Air Force flight suit with a brand-new set of patches, I rode back to the hangar. This time I was primed to make a statement. I'd never much cared for public speaking; maybe I'd never had anything much to say. But now that mikes kept getting shoved in my face, I felt no shyness in responding.

For the first time in my life, I had a message I needed to share.

"The first thing I want to do," I said, "is thank God. If it wasn't for God's love, and my love for God, I wouldn't have gotten through it. He's the one that delivered me here, and I know that in my heart.

"I also want to thank the United Nations, the United States, all the NATO countries.

When I was out there, I knew you were all behind me — I could hear you, and I knew it. And I knew that everything that could be possibly done was being done. I had no doubt in my mind about that.

"I've got a lot of respect for everybody that serves in uniform, and I appreciate everything you did to get me back here at Aviano. But at the same time, I want to thank the people who went there and risked — they say they were just doing their jobs, but they risked their lives to get me out. And those are the men and women on the USS *Kearsarge* who came in to save me.

"If you want to find some heroes, that's where you should look."

That was about it. I'd learned the virtue of short speeches in Korea, and it was a habit I'd kept, even without an ice bucket to remind me.

After the reception we repaired to the Triple Nickel's snackbar with my squadron mates and their families. My fellow pilots presented me with a Top 20 list, a la David Letterman, of why I'd finally come up on my radio to get out of Bosnia. A few of the "reasons" I liked best:

- Woke up that day and wanted to see if I was on the flying schedule
- Gave up waiting for a tow truck to pull

my jet out of a ditch
- Sonic booms kept me awake at night
- Reached the pinnacle of my vehicle-wrecking career
- Told myself all the stories I knew and was getting bored
- Found out the per diem in Bihac was only $6.50
- Didn't want to burn all my leave
- Sat in the cockpit for six days and finally figured out the jet wouldn't fly

After the reception I grabbed my mail, caught a ride to my apartment, and tried to unwind.

The following day we had a press conference in the building that housed the clubs for officers and enlisted men. A mob of reporters and camera crews had assembled, from all over, but for a while there I feared I'd have to send them away empty-handed. After taking my seat at the front, a recording filled the room with my first radio exchanges with T.O. Hanford, the beginning of the end of my accidental exile. I heard T.O.'s strong, persistent voice, and then my own — frail and plagued by static, but audibly thrilled to connect.

It was just too much for me. My shoulders started heaving and I broke down right there; I covered my face with a cloth napkin. T.O.

252

was seated next to me, and he wasn't doing much better.

"You big jerk," he said. "You made me cry on national television."

That made me laugh, but I knew I'd need some time to compose myself. Colonel Wald bought me a few minutes by taking some questions himself. The first ones were slow in coming; even the media people were choked up and flustered. They weren't quite sure what to say.

When I took the floor, I answered as well as I could without treading into classified material. Most of the questions were straightforward, but one reporter led me in a little deeper.

"Did you have a contingency plan if you weren't picked up?" he asked. "What were you going to do if help didn't come?"

"If help didn't come?" I said. I looked straight at the assembly and spoke from my heart. "I was going to *survive*."

The rest of the day flew: a debriefing at my wing commander's office, a party at the squad commander's home. I left early to flop at my apartment, where a friend stayed with me for the second night. I normally prize my privacy, but of late I'd had my fill of being alone.

On Sunday I boarded another jet with Quatro and Colonel James McGuire, the public affairs officer assigned to help me, for a longer trip: to Andrews Air Force Base in Maryland. On the way we stopped to refuel in Shannon, Ireland, where some relatives I knew — cousins on my paternal grandmother's side — came out to meet me.

Their visit added just the right note; it underlined the international character of our NATO effort in Bosnia. It wouldn't have mattered had a French or British pilot been shot down instead of me. The rescue mission would have been just as big and aggressive, and the world's prayers no less fervent.

I was an American, through and through, but I was proud of my Irish and Italian heritage. My family had been here just two generations on my father's side, and it always felt good to return to the place we'd come from.

After refueling once more in Newfoundland, the C-20 sailed over the New England coast. It was great to see American soil, but greater still to see the faces of family and friends as we filed off the plane. We were hailed by a military band, and a banner that got me where I lived:

BASHER 52
America's Been Praying
Welcome Home
Scott O'Grady

No less moving was the wordless tribute of a quartet of F-16s, soaring off from a nearby runway.

They sure knew how to make a guy feel at home.

The first man I saluted was General Ronald Fogleman, the Air Force chief of staff. Not one to stand on ceremony, I asked him for a hug — and got one from both the general and his wife, Miss Jane.

That was just the beginning. I embraced my mother and my father, my grandparents and my brother, Paul, but the longest hug came with Stacy. It seemed like we stood together there for minutes — Stacy in a billowing floral print, me in my flight suit, both of us racked by loud sobs. We were oblivious to the top brass around us. Each of us sensed what the other had been through; we were reliving the past week and rejoicing in our rescued future, all at the same time. It got to the point where our parents moved around us; I think they were afraid that we might topple over.

When we broke our clinch, Stacy said to me, "I thought if you had your cross, everything would be okay. Did you have it on?"

I pulled the little dove out and said, "I always have it on," and then Stacy laughed gleefully, a sound for sore ears.

General Fogleman said a few words, and

I added a few more, about how I'd heard the whole world's prayers — and how I'd come to trust in miracles. I walked over to a town car — with Stacy at my side, keeping me well in her sight — and wheeled out to a family reunion at a house on the base. It was a lot of fun, especially when I found my Uncle Tom in his new crew cut. I had to laugh out loud when I saw it; my dad told me that the only time *he'd* laughed over those six days was when he'd gotten a gander at Tom's hair.

That night my family and friends partied on at a local country club. The highlight came near the end, when glasses were clinked and the toasting took wing. They toasted me and the Air Force and some relatives who'd been especially helpful. People were getting back to their desserts when my seventy-nine-year-old grandmother, Dorothy Giustra, stood up and said, "I have a toast!"

Everyone stilled in expectation. Nana, as we all knew her, was a very lively and vivacious — and somewhat unpredictable — woman. She raised the glass and rang out, "To the Marines!"

That brought the house down.

I heard this story secondhand. I passed up the celebration to get some sleep at a downtown hotel, where the Air Force had reserved several rooms for my homecoming. I had a lunch date the next day, at a big white house in Washington, and a healthy portion of the large O'Grady clan would be joining me.

CHAPTER TEN

Monday morning, as we found seats in our van to 1600 Pennsylvania Avenue, Nana declared that she'd be speechless the whole time there, too nervous to say a word. We all started bawling with laughter. As far as anyone knew, Nana hadn't been speechless since Coolidge left the White House.

Sure enough, no sooner were we greeted by Hillary Clinton than Nana collared the First Lady with a story about Zachary Giustra, my seven-year-old cousin. Zack was a big Bill Clinton fan; he'd written a note to thank the president for getting me out of Bosnia "safe and sound" and to ask him about his age and his favorite color. Mrs. Clinton took the tale in, smiling. She was gracious to everyone in the family.

(Later on, a beaming Nana told President Clinton how Zack "thinks you're doing a real good job — it's too bad he's not old enough to vote." To which the president replied: "It's too bad he's not on the evening news.")

While the White House curator took my family on a tour, I met with the president and Vice President Gore in the Oval Office. There I was, sitting in one of those famous high-backed chairs that were normally reserved for heads of state. I might have been really nervous if my hosts hadn't been so relaxed and easy to talk to.

I gave the president a Triple Nickel squadron patch, to add to his collection of mementos from world leaders; the 555th would be in very fast company. I also warned him that we were going to try to "zap" the Oval Office with a Triple Nickel logo sticker — kind of a "Kilroy was here" deal.

"Give me one," the president said, "and I'll do it for you."

After an hour's chat, President Clinton led me on a personal White House tour. He had a phenomenal wealth of knowledge about the rooms and furniture and their military significance. My favorite was an antique desk. It wasn't the most elaborate piece I saw, but every U.S. treaty since the Revolution had been signed there.

I'd always been intrigued by U.S. history, but it meant something more to me now. After finding out what it was like to have no rights at all — not even the right to exist — I was less inclined to take liberty for granted.

Lunch was served in a private dining room on the second floor. There were twenty of us gathered around a long, narrow table: the president and vice president, a national security official, and seventeen O'Grady relatives and friends. The menu was fantastic: grilled vegetables, a lump crabmeat salad, macadamia- and anise-crusted lamb chops with shiitake mushrooms.

I'd come a long way from my chicken stew MRE. There was just one small problem. "Excuse me, Mr. President," I said, "if I don't eat my salad." I'd yet to regain my taste for foliage, even when it came with fresh asparagus.

By the time the cherry sherbet and macaroons arrived, we were running late; a crowd awaited us outside the Pentagon. The president and I set out for his limousine. But at the outer doorway I stopped when I saw a female Secret Service agent standing there with that death look — the one where you knew she could jab you with her pinkie and lay you out.

It so happened that this was another cousin of mine, a woman named Kerry O'Grady. I got her permission before hugging her; she wasn't a large person, but no one messed with Kerry.

In the limousine I asked the president what it was like to handle the toughest job in the world. He was unpretentious in discussing it. I found him totally genuine, a man with heartfelt intentions of doing the best he could for our country. I felt proud to call him my commander-in-chief.

The rain was pelting as we arrived at the Pentagon's riverfront entrance; a stiff-backed honor guard held umbrellas over our heads. After remarks by General John M. Shalikashvili, chairman of the Joint Chiefs of Staff, and by Defense Secretary Perry, President Clinton took his turn.

"I was tempted to say that we actually arranged this weather today, so that Captain O'Grady would know for sure that he was not going to be left high and dry. . . .

"Last week, those of you who saved one brave man's life said more about what we stand for in this country, what our values are, and what our commitments are, than any words the rest of us could utter, and we thank you for it."

A president is a tough act to follow, and as I saluted and shook his hand, I confessed that I wasn't much of a speaker. "Just go up and say three words, and they'll love it," he said.

The rain had eased while President Clinton was speaking, and now the sun broke through — it felt like the whole day had been scripted for me. As I advanced to the mike, I thought of all the people I needed to speak for. Of the hostages and prisoners of war who never made it back for any ceremony. Of the Vietnam veterans who returned to insults rather than applause. Of the peacekeepers still out there in Bosnia, for the U.N. and NATO as well as our own armed forces, working day after day in their just but dangerous mission.

"I have to tell you," I began, "that I cannot believe this response. . . . But if you'll allow me to accept all of this fanfare in the honor of those men and women who deserved it more but didn't get it, to those who suffered a lot more than I went through, to those who were POWs, to those who gave the ultimate sacrifice, both in wartime and peacetime, for their countries . . .

"If you could do that for me now, I accept all of this."

When I heard the applause, something came over me. I raised my fists high and gave President Clinton "the snakes," the ceremonial Juvat salute.

On July 11, 1995, five weeks after the shootdown, General Shalikashvili delivered an

After Action Review to the House National Security Committee. He reaffirmed that our Deny Flight commanders "had reasonable grounds to believe that Basher flight was going to be operating outside of any known or suspected SAM rings."

But "just minutes before the shootdown occurred," he said, our threat warning communications network picked up on an SA-6 presence in the immediate area that Wilbur and I were patrolling. "Due to garbled voice communications," the general went on, "the warning was not relayed to Basher flight in time for the F-16s to take precautionary actions."

The signal that reveals an SA-6 radar is very distinctive — "like setting off a gong," in the words of one Pentagon official. Whoever received that signal on June 2 couldn't have doubted what it meant, or the peril it presented. The risk was clear, but through error — human or technical or both — the message failed to get to Magic, and so to us, in time.

"I am not satisfied at this point," Secretary Perry would acknowledge, "that we did the best job in transmitting and relaying the information to the person who most needed the information."

When Wilbur and I swung north that fateful afternoon for better weather, we unknowingly set ourselves up for the slaughter. There were still clouds around us, hiding the two SA-6s as they were launched. And because the missiles came at me from due east, and at the end from directly below me, my own plane blocked my view of their course.

Had the skies been clearer, or the missiles' angle even slightly oblique, I might have seen them coming before my jet's warning system kicked in. I might have had more than four seconds' notice — the time elapsed between my target-tracking radar alarm and missile impact. With more time, I might have steered out of trouble or suckered the second missile with chaff. When they put together a $20-million fighting machine like the F-16, they make it hard to kill.

But credit should be given where due. The people launching those missiles had an ingenious plan. They knew that our NATO aircraft were cramped by airspace restrictions, making our flight paths predictable. Most likely they got a first rough hack on Wilbur and myself with a broad-beamed search radar, which our instruments wouldn't flag, since we considered it harmless.

But that search radar might have revealed our general whereabouts to an SA-6 battery, the one recently moved on the sly to southwest of Banja Luka. The SAM operators briefly illuminated Wilbur with their acquisition radar — the better to calibrate us, to see where we were — and then turned it off. A few minutes later, they used their information to launch their missiles blind, without radar, before locking me up at the end game.

The first missile may have been deflected by the jamming system in my electric counter measures pod, until it fused and blew up between the two aircraft.

But the second SA-6 beat my jamming system, like a defensive end who sidesteps a lineman and blindsides the quarterback. With my F-16 flying straight at the missile, it closed all the faster — we met head-on.

Those guys on the ground knew their stuff. They were highly trained and very, very patient; they'd staged a classic SAM trap. Except for an equally clever, well-executed rescue effort, they might have scored a political coup: the first killing or capture of an American in Bosnia.

Instead, their aggression backfired. Yes, they were able to blow a peacekeeping pilot out of the sky. But they weren't quite up to the task of bringing him in.

From the time I hit the ground in Bosnia, I blamed no one for the bug in our missile detection network. I wasn't angry or bitter. I knew we had a superior system and that we'd learn from our mistake to make it better.

And I knew, finally, that none of us is immune to the fog of war. No matter how advanced our technology, no matter how thorough our training, things will happen in combat that confound human control.

Which is where the grace of God must come in, as it came in for me.

Dramatic incidents often lead to overdue changes. In his After Action Review, General Shalikashvili declared that Deny Flight sorties would remain restricted and that future feet-dry flights would be accompanied by protective escorts. Meanwhile, NATO would continue to press the U.N. to sanction air strikes against Bosnian Serb defenses — the ounce of prevention that could net several pounds of cure for Deny Flight pilots.

Addressing the glitch that had kept me in the dark on June 2, the general announced proposals to enhance our threat warning and communications systems.

He recommended that all future combat aircrews, as well as search-and-rescue forces, be equipped with global positioning system equipment. And he pushed to accelerate the procurement schedule for an improved survival radio. Someday soon, if funding is found, our pilots could be carrying a satellite-based radio with secure channels and virtually un-limited range. A gadget like that, truth to tell, might have gotten me out of Bosnia a lot sooner.

There was also a larger lesson to be drawn from the shootdown. My experience in Bosnia, as General Fogleman noted a tour reception at Andrews Air Force Base, "reminds us that while the Cold War is behind us, we live in an uncertain and dangerous world. The readiness of our armed forces, and the quality of our people, are essential to our nation's ability to project its power and defend its interests."

My rescue, the general added, "exemplifies both the strength of America and the commitment of its people."

Amid the hoopla of the days and weeks that followed, I was often referred to as a hero.

Every time I heard that, it made me wince. I felt like I was getting eaten alive by the Great American Celebrity Machine — getting pulled apart and put back together to satisfy some network sound bite.

For the record, I don't consider myself a hero. As I see it, I was a guy in the wrong place at the wrong time. In seventy thousand Deny Flight sorties over Bosnia, only two pilots had been shot down through June 1995;

I happened to win that dubious lottery. Before the missile rudely interrupted me, I was simply serving my country, doing my job. Once the *fait* was *accompli,* I used my training to make the best of a grim situation.

That doesn't sound like a hero to me. It sounds more like a *survivor* — a fairer label, if a label is needed.

While I was growing up in Spokane, Washington, a homegrown legend named John Stockton was tearing up the basketball court at our local Gonzaga University. Stockton was and is a great player, and a lot of kids in the neighborhood idolized him. But I couldn't quite share their worshipful enthusiasm. Athletes and movie stars never tailored my dreams.

You might say that I grew up without a hero, except for one. I didn't realize who it was until my senior year in high school, when I was interviewed for my nomination to the Air Force Academy. The panel asked me who it was that I looked up to — who was my hero?

Without any hesitation, I answered: my dad. A dozen years later I feel the same way. If I could live my life with my father's honesty and generosity and humor, I'd consider myself a success.

Then I inherited a few more heroes — a

couple hundred or so — on the eighth day of June. I owe an unpayable debt — I think it bears repeating — to the TRAP team that rescued me. Whereas I'd been on a routine mission six days before, these people *knew* what they were getting into. By putting their bodies on the line and taking enemy fire, they gave me another shot at life. My door will always be open to them; they're the most beautiful people in the world.

I feel the same way about all the sailors and Marines on the USS *Kearsarge*, who rose to the occasion in the middle of the night. My heroes are the pilots in Aviano who kept me together over the radio. They're the officers who coordinated that huge airborne package out of the CAOC in Vicenza. And they're the people who played backup or support roles, like the A-10 pilots ordered to stay out over the Adriatic who were chomping at the bit to get in there — they'd jump up on the radio just to say, "Hey, we're here and we're ready to go."

Most of the world's heroes are unsung. It's heroic to dare to make a difference in the world, whether you're defending your country or fighting fires or teaching children to read.

One of the biggest heroes I've met in the Air Force is Senior Master Sergeant Frank Jenkins, a maintenance supervisor at Ramstein and Aviano. He works fifteen hours a day, seven days a week, and he never cuts a corner; he's gone from his family almost half the year. The same goes for Master Sergeant Ray Uris, who moved down from Germany to set up the Aviano life support shop. If Master Sergeant Uris wasn't so good at *his* job, at keeping our ejection seats and parachutes in top shape, I might not be here to talk about him.

At the time of the shootdown, a good friend of mine was late into her pregnancy. When she got the news that I'd been picked up, it sent her straight into labor; she delivered before I reached Aviano.

While I didn't bring a new person into the world that week, I underwent a rebirth of my own. I walked through hell for six days. I should have been killed two or three times, but I kept on walking until someone said, "Scott, you're not supposed to be here." And He reached in and grabbed me with His hand and pulled me out.

That someone was God, and those six days in Bosnia were a religious retreat for me, a total spiritual renewal. I'm not recommending near-death experience for its own sake; it's a ride I wouldn't care to take again. But I will say that my time in Bosnia was completely positive — nothing bad has come out of it. From the instant that my plane blew up around me, and I opened my heart to God's love, I felt the most incredible freedom — my joy was unbounded.

That day, five miles up, with death at my front door, I found my key to life. It took a mighty big jolt to open my eyes, but it was worth it; I knew I'd never be lost again.

I stayed on that spiritual high for a good week after my return. I could barely sleep; my mind was winning the Indy 500 and wouldn't take a checkered flag. I had so much to think about and so much to tell the world — which is why I wanted to do this book.

My priorities weren't turned upside down in Bosnia; I'd been reexamining them for quite some time before then. But they sure were slapped into line during that first week of June. By the end of it, I realized that only three things mattered in this world.

Number one was faith in God, the source of all goodness.

Number two was the love of family and friends. That love wasn't something apart from faith, nor was it a by-product. It was faith's fullest expression. We spread God's love through our caring toward others.

Number three was good health, the physical foundation for faith and love. My Aunt Ellen stayed sharp to the end, mentally and spiritually, but it wasn't enough — her body let her down, and we all lost someone precious.

Beyond that, everything was negotiable. I liked a saying that went, "Never sweat the small stuff," and almost everything is small stuff.

It is nice to find meaning in your job, for example, but the search can also consume you. I chose my calling when I was thirteen years old. I worked extremely hard my last two years in high school to get into a decent college. I worked harder still at Embry-Riddle, both in class and in my ROTC program, to pave my way into a top pilot training program. I kept pushing myself to make it into an F-16 and to perform well enough to stay there.

I did all these things and achieved my great goal, and I was totally unprepared for the question that confronted me: *Now what?* I'd climbed to the top of my ladder, and still I wasn't content. What would I strive for now? And how could I be sure it would make me any happier?

When you come down to it, a person's work just isn't that important. If you die tomorrow, what you've done for a living would be highly insignificant. No one is irreplaceable in a job. If I never returned to Aviano, Brick Izzi would find someone else to fill out his mission roster. My stand-in might do a little better or a little worse, but he'd get the job done.

I still loved flying an F-16, but if they told me tomorrow that I'd never fly again, I'd accept it without remorse. In Bosnia I was stripped of my plane and all my high-tech apparatus. I was still an officer in the U.S. Air Force, still bound to our code of conduct, but my rank couldn't shield me from a bullet. As I huddled in those woods, I didn't feel like Captain O'Grady, fighter pilot. I was just a scared guy named Scott, getting by on his wits, discovering more about himself each day. I gained a new sense of self-worth, and it had nothing to do with any medals or decorations.

I was just *me*, and I was happy in that.

If my career had come to mean less to me, worldly wealth meant next to nothing. There were many times in the woods when I would have given every penny I owned — signed it away in a blink — to be rescued. I remembered a TV commercial I'd seen about money and "success." There was this guy running around in circles and talking real fast: "I need to work harder so I can make more money, so I can buy more coke, so I can work longer and harder to make more money, and then I can buy more coke."

It was an evil, vicious circle, and you didn't have to be an addict to be dizzied by it. In my Juvat days I paid about $500 for a Dae Woo, an old, beat-up Korean car. The backseat was an archaeological dig, with layers of garbage from a horde of former owners. The front passenger door was the only one that opened; the lights and window washer didn't work at all. You could smell the exhaust as you drove — you could see the street through a hole in the floor. But all I needed was something to get me around the base, and that Dae Woo suited me fine.

Then I got to Germany with some money saved — I'm not a big shopper, still wear clothes from high school — and I wanted a machine that could hold its own on the Autobahn. So I went ahead and bought a brand-new BMW 325i: four doors, black leather interior, fully loaded.

Before long I realized I wasn't happy with that car. I got sick of washing it, and fretted over every small scratch. It was *too* nice — it got to the point where the car owned me. By the time I got to Italy, I'd decided to trade it in for some rugged, four-wheeling truck. When you got a scratch on a truck, it looked like it was supposed to be there.

I wound up selling the BMW to the insurance company after that little accident en route to Aviano. And I was right: I was happier without it.

I'm not sure about the moral to that story, but I am convinced that we are more than the sum of our material possessions. I believe that every person is a spiritual being having a human experience. That there is a life before this one and a life to follow. And that the point of our brief time on earth is to come to grips with what is eternal inside us — the part we'll take with us when we leave the rest behind.

When the Pentagon ceremony ended, it was time to take a breath. I'd gone from the Bosnian woods to the White House in four tumultuous days, with crowds of friends and well-wishers at every turn. They'd been four days to treasure, but now I needed to do something outside the public eye — something for myself.

I conferred briefly with Colonel McGuire. A few minutes later we were in a military car with Quatro and Captain Rob Swaringen, an old Panton friend from Korea, headed for my favorite place in the Washington, D.C., area: Arlington National Cemetery.

At previous visits I'd taken in as much of the vast, rolling space as I could: the neat rows of simple white stones for Civil War dead, stretching to the horizon; the columned, hilltop mansion, once home to Robert E. Lee; the eternal flame by the grave of John F. Kennedy and the small white cross nearby for his brother Robert. When I walked through Arlington, I felt the history behind it, the presence of all the men and women who'd endured such horror that we might live in freedom today.

This afternoon I had a specific pilgrimage in mind; I asked the colonel to bring us to the Tomb of the Unknown Soldier. We walked to the base of the steps leading up to the Tomb and the Memorial Amphitheater behind it. Above us, on the plaza fronting the crypt, paced the honor guard from the 3rd U.S. Infantry. The sun gleamed on the visor of his cap.

We circled around to the top, where the area was roped off for construction. After Colonel McGuire spoke to the man in charge, I stepped over the chain to the Tomb itself and knelt before its enormous cap of Colorado marble. The visitors were hushed around us. All I could hear was the click of the sentinel's heels, the slap of his palm on his M-14.

As I prayed, I thought of the four unknown servicemen interred here, spanning the wars of this century. Each one had served nobly; each had given his life — more, his identity

— to a cause he thought greater. And what had they gotten in return? No thanks or applause, no medals or parades or guest spots on TV talk shows.

But the Tomb stood for what lasted. It wasn't the reward that mattered or the recognition you might harvest. It was your depth of commitment, your quality of service, the product of your devotion — these were the things that counted in a life.

When you gave purely, I thought, the honor came in the giving, and that was honor enough.

We hope you have enjoyed this Large Print book. Other Thorndike Press or Chivers Press Large Print books are available at your library or directly from the publishers. For more information about current and upcoming titles, please call or write, without obligation, to:

Thorndike Press
P.O. Box 159
Thorndike, Maine 04986
USA
Tel. (800) 223-6121 (U.S. & Canada)
In Maine call collect: (207) 948-2962

OR

Chivers Press Limited
Windsor Bridge Road
Bath BA2 3AX
England
Tel. (0225) 335336

All our Large Print titles are designed for easy reading, and all our books are made to last.